CONCISE
LINCOLN
LIBRARY

—

EDITED BY RICHARD W. ETULAIN,
SARA VAUGHN GABBARD, AND
SYLVIA FRANK RODRIGUE

KENNETH J. WINKLE

Abraham and Mary Lincoln

Southern Illinois University Press
Carbondale and Edwardsville

14 13 12 11   4 3 2 1

The Concise Lincoln Library has been made possible in part through
a generous donation by the Leland E. and LaRita R. Boren Trust.

Portions of this book are reprinted or adapted from the author's
previously published work: his essay "The Middle-Class Marriage
of Abraham and Mary Lincoln," in *Lincoln's America, 1809–1865*,
edited by Joseph R. Fornieri and Sara Vaughn Gabbard, 94–114
(Carbondale: Southern Illinois University Press, 2008); and his
book *The Young Eagle: The Rise of Abraham Lincoln* (Dallas: Taylor
Trade Publishing, 2001).

Library of Congress Cataloging-in-Publication Data
Winkle, Kenneth J.
Abraham and Mary Lincoln / Kenneth J. Winkle.
  p. cm. — (Concise Lincoln library)
Includes bibliographical references and index.
ISBN-13: 978-0-8093-3049-2 (cloth : alk. paper)
ISBN-10: 0-8093-3049-0 (cloth : alk. paper)
ISBN-13: 978-0-8093-7999-6 (ebook)
ISBN-10: 0-8093-7999-6 (ebook)
1. Lincoln, Abraham, 1809–1865—Marriage. 2. Lincoln, Mary
Todd, 1818–1882. 3. Presidents—United States—Biography.
4. Presidents' spouses—United States—Biography. I. Title.
E457.25.W63 2011
973.7092—dc22   [B]   2011000944

In memory of Phillip S. Paludan

CONTENTS

ILLUSTRATIONS

ABRAHAM AND MARY LINCOLN

INTRODUCTION: A HOUSE DIVIDED

For a century and a half, the prevailing image of the marriage of Abraham and Mary Lincoln, among both historians and the American public in general, has included disagreement and discord between the two as its central motif. Biographers and historians have chronicled dozens of contemporary observations and even more, perhaps hundreds, of posthumous reminiscences that portray Mary Lincoln as unrelentingly demanding, difficult, and even at times disruptive as Abraham Lincoln's marriage partner and as Civil War America's First Lady. This by now well-documented discord, which was real, arose from dramatic differences between the husband and wife in personality and temperament that led Lincoln's longtime law partner, William Herndon, to label her without reservation "the wild-cat of the age." Most historians have followed suit in characterizing Mary Lincoln as difficult to live with, by turns head-strong and frivolous, fickle and resolute, extravagant and miserly, and ironically as both an asset and a liability in helping to advance her husband's career. The oft-struck comparison between the Lincolns' marriage and the national "House Divided" that helped to define it is apt indeed. Yet the Lincolns' marriage, while a "House Divided" like the Union itself, ultimately did not dissolve but persevered in spite of the continual, and during the war, escalating demands and tensions that undermined and threatened to destroy it.

There can be no doubt that the differences dividing Abraham and Mary Lincoln were fundamental. The central questions for a dual biography of this couple are how and why the two marriage partners were so different, how and why they formed such a stormy yet ultimately enduring and functional marital union, and how and why Mary Lincoln contributed to or detracted from her husband's success as a great American president during our nation's gravest trial. Like the nation that they inhabited during the entire course of their marriage, with its sectional conflict, ideological divergence, and eventual civil war, Abraham and Mary Lincoln endured personal divisions of their own that they continually confronted and struggled with but always managed to resolve and transcend. Abraham Lincoln's greatest goal as president was to preserve the Union, to ensure its continuation and indeed to prove for all the world to see that it was and should be perpetual. His greatest challenge as a husband and a father was to fulfill the pledge that defined his own marital union, the inscription on the gold band that he presented to Mary Todd on their wedding day—"Love is Eternal." In both respects, Lincoln succeeded admirably.

ABRAHAM LINCOLN AND MARY TODD

Origins

Both the Lincoln and Todd families had roots in colonial Virginia and settled in Kentucky during the Revolutionary Era. But there any similarities end. The American Lincoln line began with three Lincoln brothers who emigrated from Hingham, England, and settled in its namesake, Hingham, Massachusetts, in 1637. These Lincoln ancestors flourished, and within their first generation in Hingham sixty Lincolns were living in the town. In fact, by 1680 one-fourth of Hingham's townspeople were named Lincoln. Although they came from a long line of linen weavers, one of the original Lincoln brothers, Samuel, found linen weaving an impractical livelihood in the colonies, so he acquired some land and turned to farming, which formed the Lincoln family's principal livelihood for the next century and a half. Samuel's son Mordecai left Hingham as a young man to seek opportunity elsewhere, beginning another Lincoln family tradition of moving, usually westward, in search of opportunity. In fact, throughout their history the Lincolns proved an extremely migratory family. Over the course of six generations and two hundred years, the family line between Samuel Lincoln and President Abraham Lincoln traveled nearly two thousand miles, with each generation (including the sixteenth president) typically making two or three major moves to improve its situation. Before the advent of modern agricultural techniques, most farm families practiced the traditional policy of "escape and repeat." After depleting the soil on their farms, families would move westward to "escape" to new land, and—after a generation or so—"repeat" the process. The first three generations of Lincolns took their family through three colonies, from Massachusetts to New Jersey to Pennsylvania in search of newer and larger farms. Their sojourn in Pennsylvania, which lasted less than one generation, reinforced the future president's erroneous impression that "The family were originally quakers, though in later times they have fallen away from the peculiar habits of that people."

The family's fourth generation, a knot of five Lincoln brothers living and farming in Rockingham County, Virginia, just east of the Alleghenies in the fertile Shenandoah Valley, established what President Abraham Lincoln considered his ancestral home. During the eighteenth century, few northern settlers traveled directly west across the Alleghenies but preferred to swoop southward around this forbidding mountain barrier and cut through the Cumberland Gap into Tennessee and Kentucky. As a result, the Shenandoah River was the major route for northern families moving westward from Pennsylvania, New York, and New England. Rockingham County was the most mountainous and sparsely settled county in the Shenandoah Valley, so independent yeoman farmers who eschewed slavery and owned few slaves dominated this southern frontier area. Despite spending three generations living in Virginia and Kentucky, there is no evidence that any of Lincoln's direct ancestors ever owned slaves. Here in the Shenandoah Valley, Abraham Lincoln, the president's grandfather, married, settled on a farm near his parents' home, and raised a family of five children. This Abraham Lincoln served in the colonial Virginia militia and in the Revolutionary War and became known ever after as "Captain Abraham." The Lincolns were genuine frontiersmen and lived near the archetypical American pioneers, the Boone family, on Linnville Creek, a tributary of the Shenandoah. Lincolns mingled with Boones, and in fact the two families intermarried.

By the late 1770s, Virginia began filling up and good land grew scarce. Virginians began moving westward into Kentucky County, across the mountains, and Rockingham County, in particular, sent a cluster of settlers to central Kentucky's Bluegrass region. Daniel

Boone himself led an emigration to Kentucky in 1779, shepherd-ing more than one hundred pioneers through the Cumberland Gap along Boone's Trace, the trail that he helped blaze. Captain Abraham decided to join this huge Boone party as it moved westward. Follow-ing a family pattern, four of the five Lincoln brothers went west to Kentucky, while one of them remained in Rockingham County to inherit their father's farm. Captain Abraham sold his own farm in Virginia and bought two tracts of new land totaling 1,200 acres in Kentucky. In 1782, the entire family—Abraham, his wife Bathsheba, and their five children—moved westward to Kentucky. The Ameri-can Revolution, which was still raging on the frontier, provoked a long military struggle with Native American tribes. The Continental Congress recognized the Ohio River as the "permanent" boundary between Indians and whites, granting Kentucky to white settlers and restricting the Indians to Ohio. The Shawnees, who dominated the Ohio Valley, resisted. They reluctantly abandoned Kentucky and moved their villages north of the Ohio River but continued to attack white settlements to the south. Kentucky sent militiamen on raids deep into Ohio, burning the Shawnees' villages, killing their chiefs, and forcing the Indians still farther northward. Settled in Lexington, Kentucky, the ancestors of Mary Todd played a conspicuous role in this campaign against the Shawnees. Colonel Levi Todd led the Fayette County militia and even commanded Daniel Boone.

Unluckily, the Lincoln family arrived in Kentucky in the midst of this extended military conflict. In May 1786, an Indian raiding party, probably Shawnee, attacked and killed Captain Abraham Lincoln while he and his three sons—Mordecai, Josiah, and Thomas—were clearing a field for planting, just east of Louisville on the Ohio River. Captain Abraham died instantly. Josiah ran to a nearby fort, and Mordecai fled into the family's cabin. The youngest son, eight-year-old Thomas, simply sat crying by his dead father's side. From within the cabin, the oldest brother, Mordecai, aimed a gun through a chink in the logs and killed his father's attacker. Abraham's death, as his grandson and namesake recalled seventy-five years later, plunged his family into a life of "reduced circumstances" and, in particular, turned young Thomas Lincoln into a "wandering laboring boy."

Indeed, Thomas proved the most migratory of all the Lincolns, making six major moves during his lifetime, a trek of over 700 miles.

In later life, Lincoln aptly labeled his family "undistinguished." Although extremely migratory, they were eminently typical of the frontier families of their time. As land grew scarce in eastern settlements, eldest sons usually inherited the family farm, while younger sons were forced by circumstances to move westward to fresh lands along the frontier. Farm families traditionally employed this kind of intergenerational "step migration" as a strategy in their quest to stay together, to accumulate more land, and to pass it on to their sons. Independent yeoman families functioned best not by staying put but by moving westward to settle on fresher, cheaper, and more abundant land. This was how they maintained their independence. But this strategy meant that a frontier farm family like the Lincolns was always following the edge of westward settlement, continually breaking new ground in a new community and suffering all the attendant risks of frontier life, without ever enjoying the benefits of social development afforded the second or third generations who managed to stay behind and experience a more comfortable way of life. This was especially true for Thomas Lincoln, who lost his father Abraham at age eight and, as the youngest son, had no chance to receive an inheritance. Thomas helped to farm his family's land until he turned twenty-five and then moved on to Hardin County, Kentucky, to apprentice with one of his uncles, who was a joiner. Working hard, he was able to acquire a sizable farm of his own and married Nancy Hanks, another native Virginian, in 1806. Here, on a farm in Hardin County, which was named after a relative of Mary Todd, Abraham Lincoln was born on February 12, 1809. When Abraham was two years old, his family moved yet again to another farm on Knob Creek, the first home he could remember.

Thomas and Nancy Lincoln moved three times during their first five years together, continually looking for a better piece of land with more timber or water and a more secure title. In the fall of 1816, when Abraham was seven, his father decided to move his family out of Kentucky entirely, northward into Indiana. In later years, Lincoln cited a growing disillusionment with slavery as one of his father's motives for leaving Kentucky, and indeed the family attended a Baptist church that took a conspicuous stand against slavery. But he considered a controversy over land titles as their main reason for leaving Kentucky. Because of a primitive system of record keeping, adjacent land claims often "shingled," overlapping like so many shingles on a cabin roof, and almost one-half of Kentucky's pioneers lost their land through faulty titles. Thomas Lincoln lost his first two farms in this way, a misfortune that may well have encouraged his son's early interest in surveying as a career. Thomas now faced the loss of his third farm on Knob Creek. The U.S. government was selling land in Indiana for $2.00 an acre and securing all titles through the Congressional Survey System, a vast improvement over the traditional metes-and-bounds system practiced in Kentucky and much of the South. The Old Northwest was a region of free labor, cheap land, secure land titles, and greater economic opportunity for yeoman farm families.

One of Lincoln's relatives remembered the Knob Creek farm as "knotty—knobby as a piece of land could be—with deep hollows—ravines—cedar trees Covering the parts—knolls—knobs as thick as trees could grow." Indiana represented a decided improvement but would require the family to pull up stakes once again and start over on yet another undeveloped frontier. Thomas built a flatboat out of yellow cedar. He loaded up the family's furniture, household goods, and tools, and floated down the winding creeks to the Ohio River. Crossing the Ohio by ferry, he located a 160-acre claim—a quarter section— seventeen miles north of the river in Spencer County, Indiana. He marked the four corners by blazing trees and building "brush heaps" before returning to Kentucky to retrieve his family. Abraham Lincoln had an older sister, Sarah, in addition to a younger brother, Thomas, who had died in infancy, and the four surviving Lincolns mounted two horses and a wagon, along with two feather beds, and made a two-week, hundred-mile trek to their new home in Indiana. The Lincoln family gained three major advantages when they crossed the Ohio River into the Old Northwest. First, they left a southern slave state for a region of free labor, where farm families such as theirs could support themselves in dignity and aspire to the top of the social scale without resorting to the ownership of slaves. Second, land titles were dependable, facilitating social mobility through the secure ownership of land and the chance to accumulate more. Finally, the Wilderness Road that passed through southern Indiana reached farther westward into Illinois, eventually leading the family even deeper into the emerging Midwest with its beckoning economic opportunities, from which Abraham Lincoln, in particular, soon benefited.

The young Lincoln pictured his new Pigeon Creek home as "a wild region, with many bears and other wild animals still in the woods." Indeed, the family had to cut a road through the trees just to reach their claim in what Lincoln remembered as "an unbroken forest." Clearing this forest would occupy him for the next dozen years. Large for his age, Lincoln remembered that he "had an axe put into his hands at once; and from that till within his twenty-third year, he was almost constantly handling that most useful instrument." Thus he embarked on his fabled career as an ax-handler. Like other pioneer families, the Lincolns devoted only one day to building a log cabin, their legendary "three faced camp," and there they wintered. Eventually the Lincolns boasted ten acres of corn, five of wheat, two of oats, and one of meadow. Lincoln himself planted his own patch of pumpkins. Like many frontiersmen, Thomas Lincoln combined occupations, farming in the summer and working wood in the winter as a cabinetmaker and house joiner. He and his neighbors continued their Kentucky habits, "squatting" on the land for the first year. Then, traveling the sixty miles to the federal land office at Vincennes, he made the required one-quarter initial payment on his land claims.

After two years in Indiana, Nancy Lincoln grew sick and died of a frontier ailment known as "milk sickness." The family's cattle ate a weed, poison snakeroot, and passed on its toxins through their milk. Nancy developed a case of "trembles" and died within days. Lincoln suddenly found himself motherless at age nine. Such childhood bereavement was an all-too-common experience during the nineteenth century, as Lincoln's future wife Mary could soon testify. Until the twentieth century, mothers rarely lived to see all their children reach adulthood, usually leaving behind at least one minor child. During this period, in fact, perhaps one-fourth of all children lost a mother or father before they reached the age of fifteen. Lincoln shared the tragedy of childhood bereavement with both his father and mother, his future wife and, eventually, two of his sons. Among the five generations of Lincolns who preceded Abraham, all of them experienced the early death of either a wife or a mother. Like most Americans of his age, Lincoln therefore inherited a family tradition of parental loss, which would later help him understand and empathize with his future wife.

In 1818, the same year that nine-year-old Abraham Lincoln lost his mother Nancy in the wilderness of Indiana, Mary Ann Todd was born into dramatically different circumstances in Kentucky's largest town, Lexington. The roots of the large and influential Todd family lay in Scotland's struggle against the English crown. Rebellious Scottish Covenanters fled to northern Ireland, and many of them later emigrated to colonial America. Mary Todd's great-grandparents, David and Hannah Todd, settled in southeastern Pennsylvania in 1737 as part of this Scots-Irish immigration that populated the piedmont and backcountry with frontier families renowned for their fiery independence. Three of David and Hannah Todd's sons went to Virginia to attend a school run by their uncle, the Reverend John Todd, a Presbyterian minister, establishing the Virginia branch of the family. Serving with distinction in the Revolutionary War, the Todds rose to prominence in postrevolutionary Virginia and Kentucky. They began to intermarry with many of Virginia's "First Families," and indeed Dolley Madison's first husband was a Todd. So illustrious did the family grow that a popular adage held that one "d" was good enough for God, but the Todds required two.

The Reverend John Todd used his influence with Virginia governor Patrick Henry to win commissions for his three nephews under General George Rogers Clark in his campaign to secure the Illinois country. The most distinguished of the three brothers, John Todd, achieved the rank of colonel, rose to second in command under Clark, and earned appointment as the first governor of Illinois Territory. After the war, Colonel Todd led Kentuckians against the Native Americans and British at the Battle of Blue Licks. He died in the battle but left twenty thousand acres of land and a heroic reputation, both of which helped to sustain his family for generations to come. The stockade he erected became the nucleus and central marketplace of the future town of Lexington, named for the celebrated battle in Massachusetts that had recently sparked the War of Independence. Colonel Todd's younger brother, Levi, outdid him by attaining the rank of general. He went on to acquire seven thousand acres of his own in the heart of the Kentucky Bluegrass country around Lexington and held the office of Fayette County clerk for the next twenty-seven years. This military hero, pioneering land speculator, and influential politician was Mary Todd's grandfather. General Levi Todd and Captain Abraham Lincoln arrived in Kentucky within a year of each other, but Todd's wealth, connections, reputation, and foresight enabled him to buy land in the Bluegrass country, which made a decisive difference between the two families' respective fortunes.

To speed the settlement of Kentucky, 104 subscribers, including Levi Todd, paid a virtual army of woodcutters to chop the Wilderness Road through the Cumberland Gap, a task that took a mere twenty-two days but secured the new state's economic development for the foreseeable future. Over the next decade, Kentucky's economy flourished and its population tripled. Above all, the Todd family prospered, and an extended family of forty Todds soon dominated the social and political life of the Bluegrass region. Levi Todd worked as a lawyer and surveyor and fathered thirteen children, naming his seventh child after his brother Robert. This younger Robert, Mary Todd's father, was born in Lexington and attended Transylvania University, which his own family had helped to establish near their home in the center of the town. He studied law and was admitted to the bar, but as a southern gentleman he never practiced his profession, in part because of a glut of lawyers in the area. Robert Todd married a second cousin, Eliza Parker, daughter of another of Lexington's original founding families. Thus began a tradition of dynastic marriages that his descendants would pursue in both Lexington, Kentucky, and Springfield, Illinois. Between 1812 and 1825, Eliza Parker Todd bore seven children. The third child, born in 1818, was Mary Ann Todd, named after an aunt, her mother's only sister. Both of her parents were born in Lexington, so Mary Todd was a third-generation Lexingtonian, in striking contrast to the Lincolns, who moved two or three times in every generation.

Here, Robert Todd prospered as a bank president, state legislator, wealthy landowner, and prominent Whig. In all, he fathered sixteen children with two wives, emerging in the process as the patriarch of one of the most distinguished families in Kentucky. Lexington became an outpost of what historians have labeled the "urban frontier," a refined western community crafted in the mold of the older and larger coastal cities, with their fashionable townhouses, taverns, inns, and country estates, and boasting genteel amusements, such as horse races, foxhunts, levees, and cotillion balls. The town's leading families valued education and founded Transylvania University, the first university west of the Alleghenies, along with a law school, a medical school, and a host of girls' and boys' academies. As Kentucky's largest town and its cultural capital, Lexington truly earned its reputation as the "Athens of the West." Befitting her social class and southern heritage, Mary Todd grew up attended by—and accustomed to managing—a staff of African American slaves, including a cook, a carriage driver, a gardener, and most importantly, a nurse or "mammy," affectionately dubbed "Aunt" Sally. Indeed, slavery underlay the prosperity of the town, one-third of whose residents were slaves.

Mary Todd might well have matured and married in Lexington. She was groomed to live the same genteel life as her mother, marry well, and establish a fourth generation of Todds within the city. But the same kind of loss that her future husband had suffered, and at an even earlier age, altered her fortunes. First, she lost a brother, Robert Todd, her father's namesake, who died in infancy. Then, in 1825, her mother Eliza died after giving birth at age thirty-one. Eliza Parker Todd's sudden death left Mary motherless at age six and eventually provoked a bitter schism among the Todds. Instead of mourning for a year in proper aristocratic fashion, Robert Todd began a courtship while attending the legislature in Frankfort. Within six months, he proposed to Elizabeth Humphreys, and within a year and a half he remarried. This new Elizabeth Todd, known to all as Betsey, went on to bear nine children in the succeeding fifteen years. The Parker family never forgave Todd for his haste in remarrying, and not a single Todd or Parker attended his second wedding. Eliza Todd's children quickly learned to resent everything about their new stepmother. From thence forward, Mary Todd's outward life of comfort concealed an abiding, and at times debilitating, inner sense of loss, insecurity, and rivalry for affection and approval.

Families

During Lincoln's youth, on both the Knob Creek and Pigeon Creek farmsteads, his family lived a dramatically different lifestyle from the slave-owning urban elite that included the Todds. Farm families like the Lincolns obeyed a traditional pattern that historians label *cooperative*. Cooperative families had a strong economic foundation, in which all family members played a productive role. In this preindustrial era, most husbands and fathers worked at home, where they lived, either on farms or in small shops. Families produced most of the food and goods they consumed at home in an elaborate system of home manufacturing. Women played an indispensable role in this subsistence economy. They supervised dairy and poultry operations, made soap and candles, and above all produced cloth. Before the appearance of spinning and weaving mills after 1815, farm women made most of the clothing their families wore. They spun cotton and wool, wove cloth on looms, dyed the cloth with homemade pigments, and sewed it into clothing by hand. Through this laborious process, frontier mothers typically provided one set of clothing each season for every family member. As late as 1840, farm women produced more cloth at home than all American textile mills combined.

Until he came of age in Illinois, this kind of traditional, subsistence family was all that Abraham Lincoln had ever known. During his youth, in both Kentucky and Indiana, the Lincoln family practiced classic subsistence agriculture. When the Lincolns arrived, their Indiana farm was isolated and self-contained, a literal wilderness without neighbors, roads, or towns. The Lincoln family grew most of the food they ate and traded (literally bartered) only for the few goods that they could not produce for themselves. After joining the family in Indiana, one of Nancy Lincoln's relatives, Dennis Hanks, observed that Thomas Lincoln "Jest Raised a Nuf for his own use he

Did Not Send any produce to any other place Mor than Bought his Shugar and Coffee and Such Like." Subsistence was the best guarantee of survival in a frontier economy, and fortunately the Lincoln farm could meet most of the family's needs. "Lincoln's Little Farm was well Stocked with Hogs, Horses & cattle," another relative, A. H. Chapman, reminisced with apparent pride, as well as "a fine crop of wheat corn & vegetables." The Lincolns tanned their own leather, made their own shoes, wove their own cloth, and sewed their own clothing, all by hand. In this seasonal economy, Thomas supplemented farming with carpentry by building cabinets and joining his neighbors' houses "at odd times" during the winter. His wife ran the household and bartered with the neighbors. "Mr and Mrs Lincoln Each worked a head at their own business," Dennis Hanks remembered, "Thomas at farming—cabinet making—& hunting; She at cooking—washing—sewing—weaving, &c. &c." Nancy clothed her family in the traditional homespun and buckskin. According to Chapman, "There clothing was all made at home and the Material from which it was made was also made at home." The family grew both cotton and flax, which they "picked carded & spun with their own hands." Through a chain migration, the Lincolns encouraged in-laws and cousins from Kentucky to join them in Indiana. Soon, a knot of reliable neighbors sprang up around Pigeon Creek to engage in cooperative farming and local exchange. Surrounded by relatives, neighbors, and friends, their farm flourished, and the Lincoln family felt economically secure. Eventually the Lincoln farm boasted a surplus of "about 100 hogs and 4 or 5 hundred bushels of corn."

Within a subsistence economy such as this, widowers found it difficult to manage a household alone, especially one with children. Predictably, after Nancy Lincoln's death, the family fell into a kind of frontier squalor, and as Dennis Hanks put it, the children soon grew "wild, ragged, and dirty." In this situation, the most typical and sensible response to the loss of a wife and mother was simply to find a new one. This was a familiar practice within the Lincoln family. In the five previous generations of Lincoln men, three had lost their wives, and every one of them remarried. Pining away, however nobly, for a deceased husband or wife was simply a luxury that no farming family could afford. Fourteen months after Nancy Lincoln died, Thomas did what he must have considered the only sensible thing and went off to fetch a new wife and mother for his family. He also followed a traditional pattern by marrying a woman considerably younger than him (by ten years) and younger than his first wife (by four years). Lincoln's new stepmother was Sarah Bush Johnston, a widow from back in Elizabethtown, Kentucky, who had three children—two daughters and one son—of her own. Thomas, age forty-one, and Sarah, age thirty-one, now joined their fragmented families together. In Sarah, Thomas chose well. She immediately did what she could to make the cabin, which she found "tolerably Comfortable," into a home. She was "neat & tidy," she "Knew exactly how to Manage children, and she took a an espical liking to young Abe." The boy soon accepted her as "a good and kind mother." Thomas Lincoln's remarriage proved a godsend for the young Abraham and represented an important turning point in his life that introduced a new positive influence into his personal development.

The two families proved a good fit. Sarah gained a new father for her three children, and Thomas gained a stepson—John Johnston, at age ten one year younger than Abraham—to help work his farm. After Sarah insisted on roof repairs to keep out the rain and snow, the three boys—Abraham Lincoln, John Johnston, and Dennis Hanks— slept in the cabin's loft. The three girls slept below in a new bed that Thomas built for them. Sarah agreed that Indiana was "wild—and desolate," but she was determined to introduce a more urban standard of cleanliness into the wilderness. "I dressed Abe & his sister up," she remembered, and soon they "looked more human." She brought her own household accoutrements, including a table, bureau, and set of chairs, into the cabin and asked Thomas to put in a wooden floor. She also reignited the young Abraham's love of learning by bringing three books from Kentucky—*Webster's Speller*, *Robinson Crusoe*, and *The Arabian Nights*. Lincoln now embarked on his lifelong effort to educate himself, and his cousin John Hanks remembered fondly that when the boys returned from the fields, Lincoln "would go to the Cupboard—Snatch a piece of Corn bread—take down a book—Sit down in a chair—Cock his legs up as high as his head and read."

Thomas Lincoln was far less supportive. In a subsistence economy, many fathers hired out their sons to neighbors to contribute to their family's survival. Like most rural youths, Abraham Lincoln began hiring out at age thirteen or fourteen. Neighbor and in-law Nathaniel Grigsby remembered the boy working mostly "at hom[e] on his fathers farm" but also hiring out and working for wages on his family's behalf. He "ocaisially took Jobs of claring or making fense rails," Grigsby recalled. "Sometimes he worked on the ohio river." Young Abraham's labor was undoubtedly essential to his family's survival. For the rest of his life, however, Lincoln resented his father's insistence that he work for neighbors rather than spending his free time improving himself. As one of those neighbors concluded, Thomas "taught him to work but never learned him to love it." Lincoln's stepmother Sarah was far more sympathetic and reminisced that "Abe was a good boy; he didn't like physical labor—was diligent for Knowledge—wished to Know." Under this stepmother's influence, Abraham learned to take pride in his own self-improvement.

The Indiana frontier, Lincoln later recounted gloomily, offered "absolutely nothing to excite ambition for education. Of course when I came of age I did not know much." In the relative comfort of Lexington, by contrast, Mary Todd's father, Robert, educated his daughter to think for herself and to speak her mind. Despite restrictive gender boundaries, young Mary imbibed her father's passion for politics and developed an avid and outspoken interest all her own. A leading Whig, Robert Todd felt at ease in the headiest political, financial, and legal circles in Kentucky and associated with the likes of Henry Clay, John Crittenden, and John Breckinridge. Mary urged her father to aspire to the presidency and resolved that, one way or another, she would someday live in the White House. In the meantime, she supported Lexington's favorite son Henry Clay when he ran against President Jackson in 1832. According to tradition, the young Mary rode her pony out to Clay's estate, Ashland, and announced, "Mr. Clay, my father says you will be the next President of the United States. I wish I could go to Washington and live in the White House." Clay responded that "Well, if I am ever President, I shall expect Mary Todd to be one of my first guests." As she grew older, Mary began to dream instead of marrying a man who would become president and never hesitated to pursue such jointly personal and political ambitions openly.

The Todds were also surprisingly thoughtful critics of slavery before the sectional crisis stifled public dissent on the subject. In 1777, while serving in the Virginia legislature, Mary's uncle John Todd had advocated the elimination of slavery in Kentucky County. Later, when Kentucky first entered the Union, members of her stepmother's family proposed prohibiting slavery in the new state. Mary's two maternal grandmothers freed their own slaves upon their deaths in 1836 and 1850. Lexington boasted the Kentucky Colonization Society, which Robert Todd supported, and in 1833 the state banned the importation of any additional slaves, which received Robert Todd's vote and Mary's vocal support. From her "Aunt" Sally and other slaves in the Todd household, she gained a lifelong respect for the humanity of African Americans as individuals. Sally secretly aided runaway slaves headed for freedom north of the Ohio River and cautiously admitted Mary into her confidence on that subject. The traditional African folk tales featuring the weak overcoming the strong that Sally taught her may have left her with a strong sympathy for the underdog. Overall, her interactions with and genuine affection for "Aunt" Sally provided her with practical survival skills, as well as an effusive capacity for compassion in later life. More pointedly, one of Mary's relatives sired a son with an African American slave woman. Mother and son gained their freedom and emigrated to Liberia. Mary's knowledge that one of her own relatives was a former slave living in Africa undoubtedly prompted a greater personal sympathy for the plight of African Americans.

Just as for Abraham Lincoln, the abrupt appearance of a stepmother proved a turning point in Mary Todd's early life, but a negative one in this instance. Betsey Todd arrived with plans for a family of her own and a ready-made staff of household slaves to help her manage it. The Todds' slaves resented these newcomers from the Humphreys household. "Aunt" Sally, in particular, considered the new and younger nurse that Betsey installed in the Todd home a decidedly unwelcome intruder, fearing the loss, perhaps, of her special

relationship with Mary. Robert Todd started his second family aus-
piciously enough with the birth of a son and namesake a year into
their marriage. But when this child died, Mary lost yet another little
brother. Eventually, however, Betsey Todd bore eight more children
over thirteen years, outnumbering the original six and literally pres-
suring them to leave home early. Complicating life for Mary, Robert
Todd entered into a new business that required him to travel twice a
year to New Orleans for extended stretches, leaving his first family
without their mother or their father and at the mercy of the Humphreys. Increasingly, Mary turned to her sisters, her grandmother,
and her nurse "Aunt" Sally for solace, beginning a lifelong pattern
of overcompensating for her insecurity by demanding constant attendance, if not genuine companionship, from a wide circle of women
and, when convenient, men.

Yet another division between the two blended families centered
on slavery. Among Robert Todd's fourteen surviving children, six
grew critical of slavery and eventually sided with the Union, while
eight defended the institution and sided with the Confederacy. The
division was starkest among the Todd women. Mary and her three
full sisters all opposed slavery and supported the Union. All of Betsey
Todd's five daughters embraced slavery. A multitude of additional
frictions arose, which Mary's oldest sister Elizabeth summed up in
the simple reminiscence that "She had a Step Mother with whom she
did not agree." Robert Todd addressed Mary's discomfort by sending
her to obtain a first-rate education at the finest schools in the city.
At age nine, she began attending Shelby Female Academy, directed
by an Episcopalian minister, the Reverend John Ward, and his wife
Sarah. Ward's academy offered a thoroughly liberal education for
the daughters of Lexington's elite—reading, writing, arithmetic,
geography, history, and science—everything that a young woman
who aspired to be a mother might need to know to provide a basic
education to children of her own. Ward's "complete system of female
education" also included the *beaux arts* "accomplishments"—music,
painting, and sewing—that might help a woman acquire a husband
in the first place. The Todds paid extra for Mary's lessons in French,
considered a social asset, in which she grew proficient. (Latin was

reserved for boys and men who might make use of that language in law, medicine, or the sciences.) Mary threw herself into her schoolwork, excelled, and could be seen running the three blocks to school to start the day. At age fourteen, most girls would have completed their education, but after six years at Ward's, Mary graduated up to Madame Mentelle's boarding school. For the next four years, Mary spent the five weekdays a mile-and-a-half away at Madame Mentelle's, coming home only on weekends, suggesting that her boarding school experience was as much for Betsey Todd's benefit as for her own. Nonetheless, Mary received nearly ten years of schooling, an exceptional education during the nineteenth century, even for a daughter of the slave-owning elite.

That elite was losing its luster, however, as Mary approached adulthood. Lexington slipped into decline after its first generation or two, eclipsed by the region's growing river towns—Louisville, St. Louis, and Memphis—as the focus of trade and agricultural production increasingly shifted to the southwest. Once a major producer of hemp for baling cotton, the Bluegrass country now became a leading supplier of slaves for the more economically vibrant southwestern frontier centered on New Orleans and Natchez. Between 1830 and 1860, Lexington's population stagnated and indeed declined. Meanwhile, Louisville's population doubled during the 1840s, and by 1850 the river port overtook Lexington as Kentucky's largest city. Eventually, Lexington's economy grew dependent on the sale and shipment of surplus slaves westward. Flatboats carried them by the score down the Ohio and Mississippi Rivers bound for New Orleans, as Abraham Lincoln soon could attest personally, much to his discomfort. Indeed, when Robert Todd died in 1849, Mary's brothers auctioned off the family's longtime household slaves to help pay debts and liquidate the estate. As Lexington slowly declined, Robert Todd realized that despite all his efforts to the contrary, he could never hope to keep fourteen children from moving westward in the typical fashion of the common yeomanry. The Todds had to accept either a piecemeal migration farther west or a severe curtailment of their next generation's standard of living—or more probably both.

Westward

While Mary Todd was attending Madame Mentelle's boarding school in Lexington, Abraham Lincoln was acquiring an education of his own making on the Indiana and Illinois frontiers. Unlike Mary Todd, labor, rather than education, drew Lincoln farther and farther afield from his family. At seventeen, Lincoln found a job working on a ferry on the Ohio River and soon had earned his first dollar, an occasion that he remembered proudly for the rest of his life. After hauling some trunks aboard a steamboat for a couple of travelers, he was astounded when they each tossed him a half-dollar. "I could scarcely credit," he recalled as president, "that I, a poor boy, had earned a dollar in less than a day." At age nineteen, Lincoln traveled by flatboat all the way to New Orleans. This 700-mile journey broadened his geographical and cultural horizons, giving him a glimpse of the world beyond the confines of the Lincoln family farm, and represented his initiation into the practice of African American slavery within the Deep South.

This widening world drew Lincoln and his family yet farther westward. John Hanks, Nancy Lincoln's first cousin, joined the Lincoln clan in Indiana six years after they arrived and bought a farm next to theirs. He married in 1826 and two years later decided to move to Illinois, settling on a farm near Decatur, on the Sangamon River thirty miles east of Springfield. In typical pioneer fashion, Hanks beckoned his in-laws with descriptions of Illinois' rich prairie soil. Both of Sarah Lincoln's daughters and sons-in-law decided to follow Hanks westward to Illinois. Dennis Hanks remembered decades later that Sarah Lincoln "could not think of parting with them," and so the entire clan decided to move west to Decatur, Illinois, together.

This time, however, the family moved without Lincoln's sister. At age twenty, a year after marrying Aaron Grigsby, a member of a prominent local family, Sarah died in childbirth. By the time he was eighteen, three out of five members of Lincoln's immediate family—mother, brother, and sister—were dead. Like many resilient pioneer families, however, this fragmented family survived and indeed grew. Thomas was now the patriarch of an extended family of thirteen members, his own family and those of his two stepdaughters.

Experienced at moving, the family began to prepare for the journey several weeks in advance. They sold their farm to an in-law, Charles Grigsby, and their farm surplus to a neighbor, amassing a sizable nest-egg of almost $500. In March 1830, this Lincoln-Hanks-Johnston clan, as they thought of themselves, left for Illinois in three covered wagons that Thomas Lincoln built. Dennis Hanks recalled that "We all went—Lincolns, Hankses, and Johnstons all hanging together." James Gentry, the local storeowner, remarked years later that "I well remember the day when the Lincolns started for Illinois. Nearly all the neighbors were there to see them leave."

They settled near Decatur on the Sangamon River, where they encountered Illinois's fabled prairies and took up prairie agriculture for the first time. Traditionally, southerners preferred to farm dense woodland, which they considered more fertile than prairie land, and typically spent years clearing trees from the forests to make fields. Abraham Lincoln, for example, spent most of his boyhood between the ages of seven and twenty-one cutting down trees. Now, as the Lincolns moved out onto the prairies of Illinois, he exchanged his ax for a hoe and "broke prairie," laboriously peeling off the thick sod to reveal the rich, black soil beneath. In their first year, he and his family broke ten acres of ground and planted it in corn. Like the other pioneer families of Illinois, they discovered that the prairies were even more fertile than the woodlands. Before long, settlers preferred the prairies, realizing that they could make a farm "by merely fencing it in and ploughing—no chopping—no logging—no stumps." Farmers began pouring into central Illinois.

As he had done in Indiana, Lincoln exchanged labor with neighboring families, but this time he worked on his own account. Neighbors recollected that he "worked among the farmers, picking up enough to clothe himself." He split rails and chopped wood with his famous ax and broke prairie with a team of four oxen. According to legend, he broke fifty acres of prairie during his first year in Illinois. In a typical agreement, Lincoln split rails for John Hanks's sister, receiving a single yard of homespun cloth for each stack of four hundred rails he split. He worked until he had enough cloth, which was "richly dyed with walnut bark," to make a pair of trousers. He also exchanged labor for room and board. "His home with his father thenceforth was but nominal," fellow lawyer Henry Whitney recalled years later. "He really lived with families for whom he worked as a hired laborer." Boarding with neighbors also introduced Lincoln to his lifelong passion, politics. According to legend, the youth was plowing a field near Decatur when he "heard cheering upon 'the square,' so turned his oxen into a corner, vaulted the fence, and went to see what was 'going on.'" He listened to a Democratic speaker and then leapt onto a stump to deliver his first political speech, urging the improvement of the Sangamon River.

At age twenty two, Lincoln's search for work drew him away from his family forever. John Hanks was an experienced flatboatman and had already made a dozen trips down the Ohio and Mississippi Rivers to New Orleans. In the spring of 1831, he found work floating a load of pork, corn, and live hogs to market in New Orleans for Denton Offutt, a Springfield merchant. Lincoln had gained experience as a raftsman on the Ohio River. He and his stepbrother John Johnston joined Hanks on the journey, floating together down the Sangamon, Illinois, and Mississippi Rivers. The three adventurous youths bought a large canoe and paddled it downriver into Springfield, which Lincoln remembered as "the time and manner of A's first entrance into Sangamon County." Leaving his father's family behind him at last, Lincoln arrived in Springfield in March 1831, a self-described "strange, friendless, uneducated, penniless boy"—the son of an "undistinguished family" indeed.

Lincoln chose New Salem—although some of its residents claimed it was the other way around—as his new home when the flatboat ran aground on the village's milldam. New Salem sprang up in 1829 when two settlers built a mill on the Sangamon River about twenty miles downstream from Springfield. Only two years old when Lincoln arrived, New Salem was a typical frontier village, a cluster of log cabins on a bend in the river, providing essential services, such as milling, for several knots of settlers clustered along the timbered creek beds. While waiting for their grist, farmers had time to patronize a store, a craftsman, a doctor, or a tavern. New Salem eventually boasted the mill, a ferry, three general stores, a cooper, a blacksmith, a wheelwright, a hatter, a tanner, two doctors, and the homes of the ten to fifteen families who constituted the village. Largely self-sufficient, New Salem was, as one of Lincoln's neighbors described it, "isolated from the great world outside."

New Salem offered not only employment but the chance for an education. Growing up in Kentucky and Indiana, Lincoln had attended school for a total of only one year (in contrast to Mary Todd's ten years of formal education). Later in life, he lamented that "He was never in a college or Academy as a student". Indeed, in 1858 Lincoln submitted an entry to *The Dictionary of Congress* that included under the heading "Education" a single word—"defective." Despite his "defective" education, however, Lincoln soon gained attention and encouragement from New Salem's elders. They organized a debating society to discuss current issues and to help educate the village's young men. Lincoln attended, gave a speech, and astonished his audience with his eloquence and poise. "As he arose to speak," Robert Rutledge recalled many years later, "his tall form towered above the little assembly. Both hands were thrust down deep in the pockets of his pantaloons. A perceptible smile at once lit up the faces of the audience, for all anticipated the relation of some humorous story. But he opened up the discussion in splendid style to the infinite astonishment of his friends." Despite his want of a formal education, Lincoln clearly possessed the potential to succeed. The village elders took an interest in the young man, encouraged him to study, and provided him with a variety of opportunities.

Here, as a young adult, Lincoln embarked on an ambitious campaign of self-improvement. He may have studied briefly with the village schoolmaster, Mentor Graham, but was largely self-educated. In one of his autobiographies, Lincoln himself wrote pointedly and with apparent pride that "He studied with nobody." New Salem's settlers remembered Lincoln as a voracious reader. "Used to sit up late of nights reading," one of his friends remembered, "& would recommence in the morning when he got up." Most of his reading was utilitarian, designed to improve his mind and his prospects, although he enjoyed both Shakespeare and Burns. (His future wife, who had a thirty-five-book library in the Todd home from which to choose, was especially fond of novels.) As Lincoln later lamented—or perhaps boasted—"What he has in the way of education, he has picked up."

New Salem was also a good place for a young man like Lincoln to experiment with the wide range of occupational roles that were emerging in the free society of the North. During the six years that Lincoln lived in New Salem, he practiced nine different occupations before choosing a career. He arrived in the village as a flatboatman, floating a load of produce down the Sangamon to the Mississippi River and on to New Orleans. For a time, he helped to operate the mill that was the economic foundation of the village. By his own account, he rejected a manual occupation, blacksmithing, as well as a profession, law—he "rather thought he could not succeed at that without a better education." Instead, he settled on a career as a merchant. He spent almost two years as a clerk in one store and co-owner of another. After both of the stores went bankrupt (a misfortune that he shared with Robert Todd) he abandoned all thought of a career in business. His experiences as a merchant left him deeply in debt but also established his reputation as "Honest Abe" when he repaid every penny that he owed his creditors.

The young Lincoln now "procured bread, and kept body and soul together," as he put it, by throwing together several part-time pursuits. He split rails, ran a mill, harvested crops, tended a still, clerked at local elections, and served as the New Salem agent for a Springfield newspaper. Eventually, three government jobs—one federal, one state, and one local—helped the young Lincoln get back on his feet. In 1833, Lincoln won a presidential appointment as U.S. postmaster at New Salem. The job of postmaster was essentially a part-time position. The mails left and arrived on horseback only once a week. Most people picked up their own mail whenever they visited town to avoid paying extra postage for home delivery. As a result, Lincoln had little to do, but he held the only federal position in the village, earned the respect of the community, gained a reputation for honesty, and got to know "every man, woman & child for miles around," according to a neighbor. His next appointment, as deputy county surveyor, was another step forward. Rapid settlement of the prairie created a demand for surveyors to mark off farms, run roads, and lay out whole towns. Lincoln borrowed money for a horse and spent the next four years riding the prairie, platting farmers' claims, drawing township lines, and running roads to open up the country. He studied surveying diligently and developed a lifelong interest in geometry that he later recognized as an important element in his self-education. Surveying took Lincoln up to one hundred miles from New Salem, so he met and befriended a wider range of people. His third government job, as state legislator, was the most important of all, because it launched him into a multifaceted career in politics, government, and law.

Later in life, Lincoln proclaimed proudly that he was "Always a whig in politics." He staunchly supported the idea of an active government that would encourage economic growth, create opportunity, and stimulate social development. These were central principles of the Whig Party that was emerging under the leadership of Kentucky's Henry Clay. Lincoln had grown up in a family of Jacksonian Democrats, but soon after leaving home he proclaimed himself "an avowed Clay man." During his second year in New Salem, when he was only twenty-three, Lincoln ran for the state legislature as a representative from Sangamon County but lost. He tried again two years later and eventually served four terms in the legislature. Lincoln was a leading advocate of the Whig philosophy of improvement and in particular the economic program of his idol Henry Clay—government funded transportation, a national bank, and a protective tariff to stimulate manufacturing. Lincoln also played a key role in moving the state capital from Vandalia to Springfield, ensuring the economic growth and political importance of central Illinois.

During his first term in the legislature, Lincoln roomed with John Todd Stuart, another representative from Sangamon County. Stuart, a Springfield lawyer, encouraged his young roommate to study law. Lincoln borrowed some law books and studied them in his spare time, so even as a lawyer he was mostly self-educated. After two years, he earned his law license and embarked on the career that he practiced for the next quarter century. Law opened up many more opportunities for Lincoln. Studying and practicing law gave him an acute sense of right and wrong that guided him consistently during his political career and later his presidency. As an accomplished trial lawyer, Lincoln perfected a commonsense eloquence as a speaker and writer that served him well throughout his public life. Stuart invited him to become his law partner in Springfield, so in 1837 Lincoln moved to the new state capital to practice law. Lincoln's self-education had culminated in the ideal career choice for an eloquent young man who was so firmly committed to improving himself and his society.

The west side of Springfield's busy but unpaved public square before the Civil War. Abraham Lincoln Presidential Library and Museum.

Mary Todd arrived in Springfield in the same year that Lincoln did. Like so many other southern families, both yeomen and aristocrats, the Todds hived off westward when their fortunes began to decline, along with the city of Lexington. In 1827, the Todds began a classic "chain migration" to Springfield, and eventually only one of Robert Todd's many sons remained in the Bluegrass state. The first family member to settle in Springfield was John Todd, Robert Todd's brother and Mary Todd's uncle. He attended the Medical University of Philadelphia, in Pennsylvania, where his father had settled, and then returned to Lexington in time to serve as the surgeon general of Kentucky troops during the War of 1812. Called to Springfield through a federal appointment—register of the U.S. Land Office—in 1827, Todd became one of the town's most respected physicians. A bona fide Todd, he played a leading role in the town's economic development, political organization, and religious life. Above all, his arrival initiated a steady migration stream of Kentucky Todds that eventually made him the patriarch of a budding dynasty in Springfield.

John Todd Stuart, Mary Todd's cousin who became Abraham Lincoln's law partner in 1837, was the son of Robert Stuart, a Presbyterian minister who was born in Virginia and came west to serve as professor of languages at Transylvania University in Lexington. Robert Stuart married Hannah Todd, Robert and John Todd's sister. Their son, John Todd Stuart, was born near Lexington, attended Centre College in Danville, Kentucky, and studied law. In 1828, at age twenty-one, he traveled ten days on horseback to join his namesake and uncle in Springfield. He lived with his uncle John during his first few years in town, in a form of "sponsored migration," and eventually became one of Springfield's foremost attorneys. He served with Lincoln in the Black Hawk War of 1832 and then returned to serve his first term in the legislature. Stuart was barely a year older than Lincoln, and yet—as a Todd—he was decidedly the "senior" partner who sponsored the younger man's entree into Springfield society. Renowned as "one of the handsomest men in Illinois," Stuart stood six feet tall "with a noble forehead and large dark eyes. He was courtly and dignified in his carriage, and had an easy, affable address." He was the perfect role model for the young Lincoln and, for his own part, shrewdly recognized the seeds of success in his untutored but promising colleague.

With two of its men ensconced securely in Springfield, the Todd family began the five-year process of sending its daughters, one by one, to join them. Robert Todd's eldest daughter, Elizabeth, made a crucial dynastic contribution to the family by marrying Ninian W. Edwards in 1832. Edwards was a member of another distinguished Kentucky, and later Illinois, family. His father, also named Ninian, was a prominent attorney and chief justice of Kentucky's Court of Appeals. Just after his son's birth in 1809, the elder Ninian Edwards became governor of the new Illinois Territory and moved his family to the territorial capital at Kaskaskia. The younger Ninian Edwards maintained his family's Kentucky roots, however, by studying law at Transylvania University in Lexington, where he met and married Elizabeth Todd. When the elder Governor Edwards died of cholera, his successor appointed his son attorney general of Illinois. The recently married couple, aged twenty-three and nineteen, left Lexington for Vandalia, Illinois's new state capital.

Encouraged by Todd and Stuart or perhaps by their example, Edwards soon resigned his office and moved to Springfield to enter the private practice of law, joining Stuart as one of the town's eminent attorneys. "Tall and slender, and in manner mild and courteous," Edwards had been groomed for a distinguished career in law and politics, and he quickly fulfilled his promise. Like the Todds a dedicated Whig, Edwards fell in easily with John Todd and John Todd Stuart. By 1835, the core of the Springfield branch of the Todd family was complete—three Todd men, two lawyers and a physician, heading what was generally known in Springfield as the "Todd-Stuart-Edwards family" or, more derisively, "*the aristocracy.*"

The final link in the patriarchal family chain that stretched from Lexington to Springfield was cousin Stephen T. Logan. Logan studied law and established a practice in Kentucky but later joined his relatives, the Todds, in Springfield. Boasting an established reputation as an outstanding lawyer, Logan went into partnership with Edward Baker, one of Lincoln's closest friends. He was twice elected circuit court judge but resigned both times to resume private practice. After leaving his partnership with John Todd Stuart, Lincoln spent three years, 1841–44, working as Logan's junior partner. Nine years older than Lincoln, Logan was, like his young partner, a devoted Whig who served four terms in the Illinois legislature. Judge Logan, as he was known, ran for Congress in 1848 to succeed Lincoln, but lost what had been considered a safe Whig seat. Never much of a popular politician, Logan lost another election in 1855 and was, in Lincoln's words, "worse beaten than any other man ever was since elections were invented."

The Edwards home became the center of the Todd family circle and gained renown as the focus of Springfield's burgeoning social and cultural life. More important, it became the frontier outpost of the Kentucky Todds in Illinois. Robert Todd now sent his daughters, one by one, to board with the Edwardses, to sample Illinois society, and above all to make good marriages. The next Todd to arrive was Frances, who obeyed the Todd tradition of sponsored migration by paying $150 to board with the Edwardses, thereby escaping the disharmony of her stepmother's household. Maintaining a busy social schedule, sister Elizabeth introduced Frances to Springfield society, especially the eligible young professionals who were now gathering in the town. Frances soon met and married a young physician from Pennsylvania, William Wallace. The couple moved into a Springfield boardinghouse, the Globe Tavern, opening a place in the Edwards home for yet another Todd sister.

Conducting an elaborate chain migration, the Todds had established a secure family outpost in Springfield and then painstakingly settled sons and daughters there one by one in a process that spanned more than a decade. Through sponsored migration and strategic marriages, Springfield's Todd-Stuart-Edwards family virtually guaranteed success to each of its arriving members. The family's five Springfield patriarchs—John Todd, John Todd Stuart, Ninian Edwards, William Wallace, and Stephen Logan—numbered two physicians and three attorneys. Family, education, connections, wealth, and status knit them into the same kind of oligarchy that dominated Lexington's social, economic, and political life during its first three generations and could now dominate Springfield for generations to come. Mary Todd visited Springfield for three months during the summer of 1837, ostensibly to visit her sisters Elizabeth and Frances but also to try out the idea of moving there eventually, as well. As Betsey Todd's family continued to grow, Mary Todd's continued to shrink. She was losing her sisters one by one to Springfield and undoubtedly felt the center of gravity of her own family steadily shifting westward.

Prospects

For a variety of reasons, Abraham Lincoln had trouble finding a wife. Temperamentally, Lincoln felt uncomfortable around eligible women, preferring the company of men or married women. His rough manners and appearance appealed to the sensibilities of southern men who valued rustic simplicity and honor above Yankee refinement and dignity. But they also endeared him to older women who strove to instill a modicum of gentility into this young diamond in the rough. Surrogate "aunts," such as Jack Armstrong's wife Hannah, James Rutledge's wife Polly, and William Butler's wife Elizabeth all drew him into their family circles as a frequent and welcome visitor. In fact, Lincoln's relationship with his friends' wives generated neighborhood humor and friendly innuendo. Jack Armstrong, for example, openly joked that Lincoln had sired one of his sons, an insinuation that reputedly "plagued Abe terribly," which was of course the entire point of the jest. The jest also reveals that even Lincoln's friends considered him perfectly harmless, even a joke, as a romantic rival.

The Illinois frontier limited opportunities for courtship and marriage. Most frontiers in American history have experienced both a skewed age distribution, attracting younger settlers, and an unbalanced sex ratio, attracting more men than women. In 1840, almost one-half of all adults living in Sangamon County were in their twenties. This classic "pyramidal" age structure reflected not only the nation's youthfulness in general—the median age was only seventeen—but also the generational winnowing worked by the westward movement. Then, too, far fewer women than men settled in the county, so men outnumbered women by an imposing 24 percent. This meant that one in every five men in Sangamon County was not married and, more important, had little immediate prospect of finding a wife. In fact, one-half of all adult males were single men in their twenties, like Lincoln, and there were simply too few eligible women in their age group to go around. Throughout Sangamon County, more than six hundred men had to remain single indefinitely for the lack of an available partner.

Contemporaries understandably bemoaned the scarcity of marriage-age women in the region. As early as 1832, for example, a local newspaper cautioned that "Our present stock of girls seem in a fair way of 'being used up,' soon." As late as 1845, another newspaper declared that "Indeed, we believe, there are but twelve (we have not counted them) *marriageable* females now in this city, which has a population of 4,000 inhabitants; and, if we are not in error, eleven of these are *engaged*!" The problem was obvious: "the girls all get married a few months after they get here." To make matters worse, northerners and southerners rarely intermarried. Seventy percent of southern-born men married southern-born women. Further, Kentuckians were the most exclusive marriage partners, with one-half of Kentucky men marrying Kentucky women. Each of these cultural considerations limited Lincoln's marriage prospects considerably.

The region's unbalanced sex ratio set up a tremendous competition for wives, encouraging later marriages among men but earlier matches among women. Men had to wait patiently until their late twenties or early thirties to take a wife, but women found themselves in great demand as teenagers. Up to 1840, the average man in Springfield married at age twenty-seven. The average marriage age for women, by contrast, was just nineteen. Young men simply had to bide their time until a home, a career, and a wife all came their way. Lincoln's economic situation was a final and perhaps definitive influence. Until he could support a family through a trade, a business, or a profession, he had little hope of winning a wife. Like other men, he had to wait patiently for all three until his late twenties and early thirties. This demographic reality may have contributed to the young Lincoln's seeming aloofness or indifference toward women. Friends sometimes vied for the same romantic partners, but under these circumstances everyone involved seemed to understand and generally accepted the ensuing entanglements with good humor.

Although "young poor and awkward," and thus an unlikely candidate for marriage, Lincoln did form two romantic attachments during his brief sojourn in New Salem. Lincoln boarded with James and Polly Rutledge, whose daughter Ann was four years younger than him. Remembered poetically as "a gentle Amiable Maiden without any of the airs of your city Belles but winsome and Comly withal a blond in complection with golden hair," she was quite simply the most eligible woman in New Salem. The daughter of one of the settlement's founders, three of the village's merchants all pursued her—Lincoln, Sam Hill, and John McNamar, who was using an alias, McNeil, to evade his family in New York. As Ann's brother Robert reminisced,

"A friendship grew up between McNeil and Ann which ripened apace and resulted in an engagement to marry."

Nine years older than Lincoln, McNamar was a much better prospect to marry and head a family, owning one-half of a successful store and soon a piece of farmland in the area. Soon, however, McNamar's family called him back to New York, where he stayed for the next three years. "One of those Long interminable fevers that Sometimes occur in the East came into My Fathers family and prostrated Every member thereof except myself," he explained, "and continued for Months making victims of three of them one of whom was my Father." The couple's engagement was probably more strategic than emotional on both sides. Although still engaged to marry her, McNamar stopped writing to Ann during his three years' absence. According to the Rutledges, Lincoln and Ann began a secret courtship during McNamar's absence, which "resulted in an engagement to marry, conditional to an honorable release from the contract with McNamar." Before she could break her engagement with McNamar and make her new one with Lincoln public, however, Ann Rutledge died of typhoid fever in August 1835. When McNamar returned a few weeks after her death, he had nothing to show for his long engagement except a lock of hair, a "small Braid or Tress of Ann Rutleges Hair much worn and aparently moth eaten," as he described it decades later.

Historians have long debated Lincoln's secret engagement to Ann Rutledge, focusing on its impact on his later life and even questioning its existence. For many years, Lincoln's biographers denied that the engagement even took place. Lincoln and Ann never corresponded, even when he spent three months in Vandalia serving in the legislature. Ann's name appears in none of his surviving correspondence or reminiscences. The relationship gained public notice only after Lincoln died and he could not respond to the rumors. In an effort to reveal something new about Lincoln, his law partner, William Herndon, delivered a series of lectures in Springfield embellishing and romanticizing the engagement. Herndon's romanticized account of the engagement claimed that the grief Lincoln felt over losing Ann plunged him into a lifelong depression that he never overcame. He even suggested that Lincoln never truly loved another woman, including his wife Mary. (Mary responded vituperatively, labeling Herndon at first a "renowned scamp & humbug" and later a "wretched, drunken madman.") Pointing to the overwhelming testimony contained in reminiscences as well as Lincoln's undeniable grief, most recent biographers have accepted the engagement as fact. Indeed, Lincoln mourned so long and deeply that he suffered the first of two so-called "crazy spells" that he experienced during his lifetime. Friends were so worried about him that they hid objects, such as razors, that might tempt him to consider suicide.

In addition to reminiscences, the demographic circumstances point to the existence of an engagement. Lincoln and Rutledge were just the right age to consider marrying. When she died, Rutledge was twenty-two and Lincoln was twenty-six. In 1835, the average bride and groom in Sangamon County were twenty-one and twenty-five. Both were Kentuckians, which would have encouraged the match. Lincoln, of course, later married a Kentuckian. Her relatives reminisced that the couple planned to marry only after completing their educations, Lincoln by earning his law license, which he accomplished the following year, and Rutledge by attending Illinois College, which she was preparing to do when she died.

Rutledge most likely viewed her engagement to McNamar in strategic rather than romantic terms, especially after he apparently jilted her in the same manner that he had earlier abandoned his family, leaving her available for an emotional attachment to Lincoln. For his part, Lincoln could undoubtedly see strategic advantages to marrying a descendent of the prestigious Rutledge family of South Carolina, one of whose members was a signer of the Declaration of Independence. Boarding with the Rutledges provided ample opportunities for putting Lincoln on intimate terms with Ann. Above all, the grief that he exhibited at her death was so deep and uncharacteristic that it must have reflected the loss of a love deeply felt.

Complicating this analysis of Lincoln's romance with Ann Rutledge is his second, puzzling courtship, which he commenced just a year later. Lincoln frequently visited Dr. Bennett Abell and his wife Elizabeth, who lived a mile north of New Salem, and was in fact staying with the Abells when Ann Rutledge died. "It was a great shock to him and I never seen a man mourn for a companion more than he did for her," Elizabeth Abell recounted. "He made a remark one day when it was raining that he could not bare the idea of its raining on her Grave[;] that was the time the community said he was crazy[;] he was not crazy but he was very disponding a long time." A year later, Abell devised a plan to return to Kentucky, fetch her sister Mary Owens, and arrange a marriage with Lincoln. She doubtlessly had several motives—making a good match for her sister, attracting her from Kentucky to New Salem, and distracting Lincoln from the shock of Rutledge's death.

Lincoln had already met Mary Owens three years earlier and, by his own account, considered her "inteligent and agreeable." He was therefore "well pleased with the project," so when Owens reached New Salem, he obligingly commenced a courtship. Hailing from a wealthy and aristocratic Kentucky family, Owens expected Lincoln to extend all of the niceties of a genteel courtship, something she soon found him entirely unable—or at least unwilling—to do. Lincoln quickly proved an inattentive and even inconsiderate suitor. When riding across a dangerous creek, for example, Owens noticed Lincoln "never looking back to see how I got along; when I rode up beside him, I remarked, you are a nice fellow; I suppose you did not care whether my neck was broken or not. He laughingly replied, (I suppose by way of compliment) that he knew I was plenty smart to take care of myself." As she remembered three decades later, "I thought him lacking in smaller attentions." When Owens attempted to test Lincoln's feelings for her, he came up short. She deliberately missed an appointment with Lincoln and expected him to follow her to the house of her cousin, Mentor Graham. Instead, Lincoln refused and rode back sullenly to New Salem. These episodes prompted Owens to confide to Lincoln that "You would not make a good husband Abe." Later, she reflected "not that I believed it proceeded from a lack of goodness of heart, but his training had been different from mine, hence there was not that congeniality which would have otherwise existed."

Misreading Owens's emotions, Lincoln pursued the courtship. "I mustered my resolution and made the proposal to her direct," he recounted later, "but, shocking to relate, she answered, No."

Interpreting the refusal as another "test" and therefore a challenge, Lincoln persisted. "I tried it again and again, but with the same success, or rather with the same want of success." Too socially sensitive, he was devastated, "mortified, it seemed to me, in a hundred different ways." Misinterpreting his own situation, Lincoln believed that Owens considered him too humble to make a worthy mate. Instead, Owens merely wanted a more considerate and attentive husband. "Abe was mistaken in his guesses," according to Owens's cousin, "for wealth Cut no figure in Miss Owens Eyes." Owens herself put it simply: "Mr. Lincoln was deficient in those little links which make up the great chain of womans happiness." Herndon agreed that "Lincoln had none of the tender ways that please a woman." Lincoln clearly viewed his proposed marriage to Owens in entirely strategic rather than emotional terms. Still, the experience of such a public courtship and such a humiliating rejection left him thoroughly embittered. "I have now come to the conclusion never again to think of marrying," he wrote abjectly, "and for this reason; I can never be satisfied with any one who would be block-head enough to have me."

The contrast with his emotional relationship with Ann Rutledge could not have been more striking. His proposal to Mary Owens was as passionless as possible for a man who was contemplating marriage. As a traditional, strategic courtship, it originated through the efforts of a well-meaning matchmaker, had the blessing of the bride's family, took place under the surveillance of a watchful community, and evoked little emotion from either party. Lincoln solicited a coldly rational response, posing only his poverty and not his want of passion as an objection to the match. For her part, Owens expected Lincoln to observe the formalities of a traditional courtship, going through the motions, so to speak, of a well-thumbed etiquette book or romance novel. Even if consummated, the match would have been a mere marriage of convenience.

Lincoln's relationship with Ann Rutledge, by contrast, was a true romance, calling forth an overwhelming passion on the part of the man who could not publicly proclaim his love and then tragically lost his lover. In this sense a more modern relationship, it breached the conventions of polite society by endangering Ann's family, violating her betrothal to another man, and taking place in strict privacy, indeed secrecy. Simply put, in New Salem the youthful Lincoln pursued two ill-fated engagements out of entirely different motivations. His public courtship of Mary Owens was loveless yet convenient. His private romance with Ann Rutledge was impassioned yet decidedly inconvenient for everyone involved. Yet both experiences left him embittered. Despite his resolve "never again to think of marrying," he needed to forge a connection that occupied a middle ground somewhere between these two agonizing extremes.

One month after he was admitted to the bar, Abraham Lincoln and his new law partner announced to the world that "J. T. Stuart and A. Lincoln, Attorneys and Counsellors at Law, will practice, conjointly, in the Courts of this Judicial Circuit.—Office No. 4 Hoffman's Row, up stairs. Springfield, april 12, 1837." Three days later, he left the dying village of New Salem behind him and rode the fourteen miles to Springfield on a borrowed horse, to join "his old friend, Stuart," in the practice of law. Lincoln's first task on reaching Springfield was to locate a place to live. Just as in New Salem, most men in Springfield were boarders. His immediate need was a bed to sleep in, so his first stop was a cabinetmaker's shop, where he contracted to have a bedstead constructed. Next, he headed to Abner Ellis's general store to buy bedding—"mattress, blankets, sheets, coverlid, and pillow." Joshua Speed was a partner in the store and was clerking there on the day that Lincoln walked in.

Speed was twenty-two, five years younger than Lincoln, when they met. A fellow Kentuckian, he was born into a wealthy family on a plantation near Louisville. His father, John Speed, was a judge, a planter, a substantial landowner, and the owner of more than seventy slaves. His family educated Speed in private schools to prepare him for a professional career, but he decided to strike out on his own. He was a clerk for two or three years in the largest mercantile house in Louisville and then moved to Springfield in 1835, where he spent the next seven years working as a merchant. Despite conspicuous differences in their family backgrounds (like Mary Todd, Speed hailed from the slave-owning planter class, Lincoln from the independent yeomanry), the two shared many similarities and hit it off immediately. Lincoln may have seen something of himself in the young store clerk who looked into the future with such optimism. Both were Kentuckians who had come to Springfield alone after rejecting the career paths of their fathers. Both were ambitious young men who aspired to succeed while working with senior partners who were already established in Springfield. Both were confirmed Whigs. And both were at sea amid the bubbling social turmoil of the burgeoning boom town. Lincoln was, in Speed's words, "almost without friends." The two became instant companions. Sixty years later, Lincoln's son Robert called Joshua Speed "the most intimate friend my father ever had." In fact, Lincoln's wartime secretaries and eventual biographers, John Nicolay and John Hay, singled Speed out as "the only—as he was certainly the last—intimate friend that Lincoln ever had."

Speed was already familiar with Lincoln, whose reputation as a public speaker preceded him to Springfield. "I had not seen him for the first six months of my residence there," Speed remembered, "but had heard him spoken of as a man of wonderful ability on the stump." The young clerk had first heard Lincoln speak while he was running for reelection to the legislature in 1836. Like most of Lincoln's acquaintances throughout his life, Speed was initially deceived by the young man's appearance, finding him "a long, gawky, ugly, shapeless, man." But Lincoln's simple eloquence soon won him over. "I remember that his speech was a very able one" that "produced a profound impression." Simply put, "The Crowd was with him." And so was Speed.

Decades later, Speed recalled that fateful Saturday in April when "Lincoln came into the store with his saddle-bags on his arm." Learning that the bedding would cost $17, Lincoln confided that "I have not the money to pay." Speed remembered that "As I looked up at him I thought then, and think now, that I never saw a sadder face." He suggested that Lincoln share his room above the store. "He took his saddle-bags on his arm, went up stairs, set them down on the floor, and came down with the most changed countenance. Beaming with pleasure he exclaimed, 'Well, Speed, I am moved!'"

Like most boom towns, Springfield attracted more than its share of young, single men. Fully 60 percent of them were in their twenties.

Lincoln's age group, twenty-five to thirty, was the most numerous, comprising an astounding one-third of all adult men in Springfield. Lincoln and his hapless peer group confronted a discouraging sex ratio of 2.6 men for every woman. Put simply, between two and three young men competed for every woman of roughly the same age. This discouraging sex ratio held tremendous consequences for Springfield's youths, putting a premium on both economic opportunities and marriage partners. But it made the town an ideal locale for a young woman, especially one who possessed family connections and social graces, to find a husband.

Mary Todd arrived in Springfield in that same spring of 1837 to visit her eldest sister Elizabeth Edwards and her husband Ninian. There she joined her older sister Frances, who was living in the Edwards home as a boarder while socializing and looking for a husband. Ensconced in their house on "Aristocrat's Hill," as it was known, the Edwardses introduced Mary to Springfield society. Throughout the summer, she engaged in the whirl of dances, parlor games, and political debates that enlivened the new state capital. A bachelor of the period noted "the many parties, Balls sociables, accidentals, and candy pullings and last and least the sewing societies" that occupied the townspeople. Caught up in the summer's social scene, Mary Todd returned to Lexington quite reluctantly in the fall.

During her absence, her sister Frances made an excellent match, marrying one of the town's leading physicians, William Wallace. Wallace was born in Lancaster County, Pennsylvania, and earned a medical degree in Philadelphia. At age thirty-four, he settled in Springfield, where he practiced medicine for the next twenty-five years. After marrying Frances Todd in 1839, Wallace became one of Abraham Lincoln's closest personal confidants. The Lincolns honored him in the naming of their third son—Mary's favorite—William Wallace Lincoln, the beloved Willie. Like several of Abraham Lincoln's in-laws, Wallace became a Democrat during the 1850s, but at Mary's behest President Lincoln appointed him paymaster of volunteers in Springfield during the Civil War. Frances Todd's departure from the Edwards home opened a spot for Mary, who promptly seized this opportunity to escape her stepmother Betsey by moving to Springfield. In 1839, twenty-one-year-old Mary Todd left Lexington behind her forever and moved in with the Edwardses to grace Springfield's social scene and to look for a husband of her own.

The Edwardses' location, both geographical and social, was perfect for this transplanted Lexingtonian. Their brick home on "quality hill" attracted the wealthiest and most powerful Springfielders, particularly the town's rising Whig elite of young professionals, who provided a surplus of marriageable merchants, physicians, and lawyers. Moreover, every legislative session welcomed promising eligible men from across Illinois to the new state capital. The Edwardses cultivated their "Coterie" of dependable social partners with overlapping business, family, and professional connections and enough lively wit and spending money to keep the town's few eligible ladies constantly entertained. For her part, Mary received a $120 annual allowance from her father, which went toward a suitable wardrobe and all the accoutrements she would need to attract and enamor a worthy husband, a judicious investment indeed in the Todd family's future.

MR. AND MRS. ABRAHAM LINCOLN

Marriage

They met at one of the most anticipated social events in the town's history, a cotillion at the new American House held in December 1839 to celebrate the convening of the first legislative session in the new state capital. As one of the Assembly's Whig leaders, Abraham Lincoln was named a "manager" of the event, which likely amazed and amused him beyond measure but undoubtedly impressed Mary Todd. Although shrouded in some mystery and a great deal of historical controversy, their courtship probably began during the first three months of 1840 but was forced to subside, with Lincoln campaigning for William Henry Harrison (and serving as one of his electors, which imposed extensive campaign duties), riding the Eighth Circuit (which he did regularly for up to ten weeks at a time), and on top of it all serving in the state legislature. Historians have fiercely debated the circumstances of Mary Todd's courtship of Abraham Lincoln as well as the couple's engagement and marriage. Social customs among the middle and upper classes of the day dictated that courtship take place within the aegis of the woman's family and even with their permission. In this patriarchal society, suitors "came calling" only after receiving an invitation from one of the men in the household. The Lincoln-Todd courtship therefore had the blessing, at least initially, of Elizabeth and Ninian Edwards and took place in the parlor of their imposing, two-story brick home. "Many courting couples throughout the nineteenth century continued to seek consent from the young woman's parents," according to historian Karen Lystra. "Scant attention, however, was paid to the young man's family. Nineteenth-century men enthusiastically supported the value of familial independence." Indeed, Thomas and Sarah Lincoln never met Mary Todd, either before or after her marriage to their son. The Edwardses, however, felt a keen responsibility to make a good match for Mary Todd, just as they had helped Frances Todd marry well and would eventually help Mary's younger sister Ann find an equally suitable husband (Springfield merchant Clark Smith). They probably would have considered any romantic union acceptable as long as it contributed to the Todd family's strategic quest to forge broader social and economic connections. Ninian Edwards later admitted that he had "policy reasons" for encouraging the courtship, hoping to bind the promising young Lincoln more firmly within the family's social and political orbit.

Like most of the eligible women in the town, Mary Todd entertained multiple suitors, including Lincoln's political rival Stephen Douglas. Sometime during 1840, however, Abraham Lincoln and Mary Todd discreetly made plans to marry. During this era of family transition, courtship was growing in complexity. As both parental authority and economic motivations for marrying declined, couples expected to cultivate an emotional intimacy during an extended period of betrothal, a process of "disclosing and explaining the self," in Lystra's words, during which the couple would find ways to explore their true feelings and test each other's character. The male ideal of dignified self-composure prompted women to insist on—or engineer—long, drawn-out engagements to allow more time to explore their prospective husbands' suitability. Glib and emotional, Mary Todd divulged an outpouring of confidences to her suitor, but Lincoln was reluctant and possibly even unable to reciprocate. "Mary was quick, lively, gay—frivalous it may be," according to her sister, Elizabeth Edwards. Lincoln, she believed, "Could not hold a lengthy Conversation with a lady—was not sufficiently Educated and intelligent in the female line to do so." Yet he was fascinated with the lovely young woman who poured out her heart to him. "I have happened in the room where they were sitting often & often Mary led the Conversation," her sister recalled. "Lincoln would listen & gaze on her as if drawn by some Superior power, irresistably So: he listened—never Scarcely Said a word." As many observers have since remarked, Mary was clearly looking for a good listener.

Above all, standards of courtship and marriage were undergoing a dramatic transition. Just as family life in general was shifting from an economic to an emotional foundation, women began demanding a greater emotional investment from suitors during courtship. The traditional, "strategic" marriage had joined a couple together for the mutual economic advantage of their respective families. Women sought husbands whose economic positions would enhance the fortunes of their families as well as their own. Parents therefore exerted a strong and sometimes definitive influence over the choice of marriage partners, and prospective mates sought the blessing if not the permission of their parents. Traditionally, a man visited his prospective father-in-law to ask his permission to marry his daughter even before discussing the subject with his intended bride. In a more than symbolic gesture, fathers literally "gave away" their daughters on their wedding day. As parental authority declined, however, marriage began evolving into a union of two individuals rather than two families. Couples began forming emotional bonds that superseded and sometimes even flouted economic considerations. The newly emerging "companionate" marriages put a premium on emotional compatibility, transforming courtship into an often turbulent period of personal testing and emotional turmoil.

Despite Lincoln's fascination, the couple had a falling out in early 1841. After Lincoln's death, William Herndon devised a compelling but dubious story in which his law partner left his fiancée standing at the altar on January 1. The Edwardses claimed that they changed their minds about Lincoln and discouraged the match. More likely, both members of the couple felt unready to marry, and the parting was a mutual if reluctant decision. Indeed, courtships of this period were typically fraught with anxiety. "Men hesitated to commit themselves to marry—even at some date in the indefinite future," according to historian Ellen Rothman, "until they felt emotionally ready and could be sure of acquiring the necessary financial resources." Not only

Lincoln but Mary Todd likely felt unsure on both counts. "When the courtship drew to a close," Rothman observed, "even the most confident women were gripped by intense anxiety." Courting couples typically endured at least one crisis precipitated by the prospective bride's demand for a clear sign of an emotional commitment on the part of her suitor. "Women threw large and small obstacles in the path of the courting male," Lystra observes, "to measure the depth and intensity of his romantic love." Biographers have suggested that Lincoln's genuine interest in another woman (Matilda Edwards, Ninian Edwards's cousin) and Mary Todd's feigned attentions to another man (Edwin Webb, like Lincoln a lawyer and legislator) strained the relationship and led to the breach.

For a year and a half, from early 1841 until late 1842, Abraham Lincoln and Mary Todd maintained a cordial distance. Mary wrote to her friend Mercy Levering that Lincoln "deems me unworthy of notice, as I have not met *him* in the gay world for months." Longingly, she confided, "I would that the case were different, that he would once more resume his Station in Society." At the same time that the couple broke off their engagement, Joshua Speed moved back to Kentucky, and Lincoln's sense of loss and isolation precipitated his second and final "crazy spell." Grieving over his broken engagement in a way that was much more reminiscent of his feelings for Ann Rutledge than for Mary Owens, Lincoln confided in John Todd Stuart that "I am now the most miserable man living. If what I feel were equally distributed to the whole human family, there would not be one cheerful face on the earth. Whether I shall ever be better I can not tell; I awfully forebode I shall not." Hinting darkly at suicide, Lincoln concluded that "To remain as I am is impossible; I must die or be better, it appears to me." Feeling the sting of his sister-in-law's unhappiness, perhaps, Ninian Edwards called Lincoln "crazy as a *Loon*." He neglected his duties in the legislature, was reported as ill, and finally missed an entire week. Meanwhile, his friend Speed had embarked on a tentative courtship of his own, and Lincoln paid him an extended visit between August and November 1841, giving the pair a chance to commiserate. When Lincoln returned to Springfield, he wrote a series of letters advising Speed about his romance, reminding

Speed pointedly that "you know the Hell I have suffered on that point." By February 1842, Lincoln could objectively advise Speed that "I am now fully convinced, that you love her as ardently as you are capable of loving," while perhaps believing the same thing of himself.

The earliest known photograph of Mary Lincoln, four years into her marriage, at around age twenty-eight; daguerreotype made by Nicolas Shepherd in 1846. Library of Congress.

Lincoln's reconciliation with Mary Todd occurred unexpectedly yet, significantly, within a political setting. Encouraged by the wife of Simeon Francis, editor of the *Sangamo Journal*, the couple began meeting at the Francises' home, away from the now jaundiced gaze of the Edwards family. During the summer of 1842, the newly re-united couple heedlessly hatched a plot to carry their mutual political interests into the pages of the *Journal*. After the collapse of the State Bank of Illinois in February, the state auditor, James Shields, began refusing its bank notes as payment for taxes. Whigs pilloried Shields, a rising young Democrat, and Lincoln and Mary Todd could not resist joining in. Together with Mary's best friend, Julia Jayne, the couple planted a series of letters in the *Journal* that lampooned Shields. Known as the "Rebecca Letters" after their pseudonymous author, they caricatured Shields with a merciless wit that only Abraham Lincoln could summon. When Shields demanded to know the identity of the author, Lincoln gallantly took sole credit for the insults to preserve the women's honor. Shields promptly insisted that Lincoln defend his own honor and challenged him to a duel.

The duel with Shields posed a real threat to both men's lives. Lincoln selected broadswords and seemed determined to defend himself. "I did not intend to hurt Shields unless I did so clearly in self-defense," he later told Herndon. "If it had been necessary I could have split him from the crown of his head to the end of his backbone." To maintain his "reverence for the law," however, the lawyerly Lincoln agreed to cross the Mississippi River to Missouri, where dueling was legal, to face off against Shields at a popular dueling ground named Bloody Island. At the last moment, John J. Hardin, a fellow Whig and Mary Todd's relative, convinced Shields to withdraw the challenge in a compromise that allowed both men to save face. But the "duelling business," as Lincoln called it, was infectious. Shields soon challenged William Butler, one of Lincoln's seconds, to what Lincoln gleefully labeled "duel No. 2." A third duel loomed when one of Shields's seconds challenged another Lincoln ally. Like duel No. 1, however, the other two duels ended peaceably. Ironically, two decades later Lincoln appointed Shields brigadier general in the Union army.

Often viewed as a comedy of errors that simply got out of hand, in fact the Shields Affair was instrumental in reuniting the quarreling couple. Writing the Rebecca Letters resembled the kind of close collaboration that would bind the Lincolns together in the central preoccupation of their married life, advancing Lincoln's political career. Their publication empowered Mary Todd by granting her a political voice that she had never enjoyed before and never would again. Finally, the duel allowed Lincoln to demonstrate his emotional commitment to Mary Todd by defending her honor in a way that left his own intact and in fact enhanced it.

With the crisis of commitment overcome to Mary's—if not her family's—satisfaction, the couple decided to marry in November 1842. Weddings of this period exuded simplicity. Large church weddings gained favor only with continued urbanization, and honeymoons were unknown until transportation improved. "Most couples were married by a minister, at the bride's home, in the presence of a small group of friends and relatives," according to Ellen Rothman, and she might have been describing the Lincolns'. The couple's original plans called for Episcopal minister Charles Dresser to marry them at his home. "Mr and Mrs Edwards, knew nothing of the wedding until the morning of the day," a close friend recalled. When Abraham Lincoln bumped into Ninian Edwards and casually mentioned the wedding, the Edwardses expressed surprise but insisted that the ceremony take place in their home. This near elopement emphasizes the couple's determination to contract their own marriage and control their own futures. "Only meager preparations could be made on so-short notice," one of the participants reminisced, "& only a few friends were present." (A "few," in the context of Springfield's frenetic social scene, meant thirty.) Mary's bridesmaids were her best friend, Julia Jayne, who later married future senator Lyman Trumbull, and Anna Rodney, a grandniece of Caesar Rodney, a signer of the Declaration of Independence. Lincoln's groomsmen, corralled literally hours before the ceremony, were two Whig friends from his bachelor days, James Matheny and Beverly Powell. Decades later, Matheny still remembered "Old Parson Dresser in clerical robes" and "a perfect hush in the room as the ceremony progressed." Both of the betrothed must have felt mixed emotions. Legend holds that when asked where he was going that day in his best clothes, Lincoln answered, "To hell." For her part, Mary had been known to refer to marriage ungenerously as "the *crime of matrimony*" and once asked, "why is it that married folk always become so serious?" In fact, the couple seemed entirely comfortable with their long-awaited decision to marry. A week later, Lincoln was back at work, concluding a letter to a client by observing, "Nothing new here, except my marrying, which to me, is matter of profound wonder."

Like many newlyweds, the Lincolns spent their first year of married life together as boarders. In fact, they rented the same room in the Globe Tavern that Frances Todd Wallace had occupied with her husband after their wedding. Their room, all of their meals, and their washing cost them eight dollars a week. Accustomed to both the comfort and social status embodied in the Edwardses' two-story brick home on Aristocrat's Hill, Mary Lincoln suffered a precipitous decline when she moved into the eight-by-fourteen-foot room in the Globe. After five years of sleeping with Speed, boarding with the Butlers, and sometimes stretching out on the couch in his law office, however, Abraham Lincoln undoubtedly viewed the simple room he shared with Mary as a decided improvement.

As a very public place, the Globe violated Victorian standards, forcing the couple into a close intimacy with the neighbors with whom they shared meals in the common dining room. Run by George Washington Spottswood, reputed grandnephew of the first president, the tavern adjoined a livery stable and accommodated up to thirty guests at a time. The Globe provided a decidedly masculine environment with strong political overtones. Located a "few rods west of the State House," it was literally a tavern and a haven for Whigs during the legislative season. Lincoln had attended many a "jollification" there with his political cronies. In 1837, Whigs held a banquet at the hotel to congratulate the Long Nine for bringing the state capital to Springfield. After one noteworthy bash, Democrats jeered that "It took Spotswood half of the next day after the revel to *clean the house*." Like many of the era's taverns, the Globe also did double duty as a polling place on election days. More a hotel than a boarding house, the Globe housed quite a few visitors to town, mostly single men but also a few couples with children, and travelers visiting the state capital from Vandalia, Jacksonville, and even St. Louis. Abraham Lincoln undoubtedly enjoyed the male camaraderie of the tavern, but his frequent absences likely left Mary cringing at the mere thought of entering the dining room by herself.

Couples who married in Springfield generally waited two years before starting a family. Older than the average bride and groom, Mary by five years and Abraham by six, the Lincolns did not delay childbearing. Three days shy of nine months after their wedding, Mary Lincoln bore the first of four sons. Lincoln's ancestors traditionally named eldest sons after their paternal grandfathers. Thomas Lincoln, of course, honored his own father by naming his first son Abraham. As in many other respects, Abraham Lincoln eschewed family tradition when the newly married couple decided not to honor his father but rather Mary's. Indeed, most Americans by this time were abandoning the practice of naming sons after grandfathers. The naming of Robert Todd Lincoln was therefore a quaint tribute to the family patriarch and was likely an attempt on Mary's part to ingratiate herself with her father, which she had attempted to do repeatedly after her mother died. Abraham Lincoln felt no similar impulse toward his own father. Symbolically, the name signified the boy's inclusion in the prestigious Todd family, which Lincoln undoubtedly considered a superior legacy for his son. In fact, before the end of the year, Robert Todd trekked to Springfield and gave his blessing, along with generous financial support, to the fledgling family. According to family tradition, he intoned with pride, "May God bless and protect my little namesake."

A few months later, the couple moved into a more comfortable home, renting a cottage with four rooms on Fourth Street. A year and a half after their wedding, the Lincolns at last purchased a house. In 1839, the Reverend Charles Dresser, who had married the Lincolns, built a five-room, one-and-a-half-story house to accommodate his wife and two children. When he fell into debt, Dresser decided to sell the house. In May 1844, the Lincolns cobbled together some gifts from Robert Todd and a piece of land they owned with Stephen

Logan and purchased the Dresser house for $1,500. Significantly, Lincoln's Todd family connections, not his own, made this final transition to middle-class respectability possible. Located on a one-eighth-acre lot at the corner of Eighth and Jackson, it was home to the family for the next sixteen years. Only six blocks from Springfield's central square, their new home nevertheless stood on the edge of town. Behind the house sat a woodshed, where Lincoln put his years of experience as a rail-splitter to good use by chopping wood for the home's fireplaces and kitchen stove. Past the privy lay an open field in which Lincoln pastured his horse and the family's milk cow. The house was a convenient walk from Abraham Lincoln's law offices and the grocers, dry goods stores, and druggists that Mary Lincoln frequented on her daily rounds.

Society

Abraham Lincoln and Mary Todd formed their family during an extraordinary and unique period in American history. The early nineteenth century witnessed a dramatic transition within the institution of marriage, indeed within the American family itself. The economic boom of the 1830s promoted rapid industrialization and urbanization. The budding factory system began calling men from farms to cities and drew them away from their homes as industrial workers, managers, merchants, clerks, and professionals. Traditional family patterns changed as a middle class of nonmanual workers emerged in western cities. Farm families stopped producing most of the goods they consumed, growing cash crops for sale in a commercial market and purchasing the necessities they once had made at home. Significantly, industrialization came first in the textile industry, freeing farm women from the endless cycle of spinning, weaving, dyeing, and sewing the fabric that clothed their families. As a western state, Illinois industrialized relatively late, but distinct middle and working classes began to emerge during the 1830s and 1840s, just as Abraham Lincoln and Mary Todd arrived, courted, and married. Most noticeably, agriculture declined dramatically as the foundation of the state's economy. In 1840, farmers represented 85 percent of Illinois's workforce, 65 percent in 1850, and a minority, just 39 percent, in 1860. The first manufactured goods appeared in general stores in Chicago and St. Louis during the 1830s, and farmers began trading for them on their twice-yearly trips to market. In old age, one Illinois farmer's daughter remembered her father returning from Chicago with factory-made cloth and announcing triumphantly, "Wife and daughters, store away your loom, wheels, warping bars, spool rack, winding blades, all your utensils for weaving cloth up in the loft. The boys and I can make enough by increasing our herds and driving them to Chicago for sale." Freed forever from the constant drudgery of spinning, weaving, and sewing, "The girls clapped their hands with delight."

In short, textile production increasingly left homes for factories. In 1832, a textile mill opened eleven miles west of Springfield to card, spin, and weave wool. Families could now shear their sheep and have their wool carded, spun, and woven into cloth either for cash or for a portion of the cloth. John Hay Sr., father of Lincoln's future White House secretary, opened a cotton factory right in Springfield, employing working-class boys aged ten to twelve, along with blind horses, to run his mill. Gradually, the work of textile production passed from middle-class girls to working-class boys, from homes to factories. Meanwhile, the middle class—practitioners of productive but nonmanual occupations, primarily merchants, professionals, and public officials—increased from a mere 4 percent of the state's employed men in 1840 to 5 percent in 1850 and 9 percent in 1860. During the Civil War, about one-tenth of Illinois families were middle class.

Middle-class men began leaving home to go to work every morning—a process that historians have labeled the "separation of home and work"—and therefore gained visible status as the "breadwinners" in their families. Married women stayed home, and their primary role was maintaining the household for the benefit of their husbands and children. In short, they became "housewives." Housekeeping, and especially cooking, became a science, and middle-class women turned nervously to a deluge of new publications—domestic manuals and cookbooks, as well as novels and magazines—to learn its arcane mysteries. New standards of cleanliness emerged to occupy housewives during the long days while their husbands labored in factories, shops, and offices. Above all, housewives were expected to spend their husbands' salaries wisely, and families, particularly women, became consumers rather than producers. Like their mothers, middle-class children also lost their productive functions. Parents no longer passed on land to their children as future farmers but instead educated them for eventual middle-class careers of their own. As a result, children were no longer productive and reverted from economic assets into economic liabilities until they reached adulthood.

The North underwent a "market revolution." During Springfield's early years, families had raised their own food in their backyards. As a flourishing lawyer, Abraham Lincoln had kept a backyard garden and milked his own cow. Soon, however, Springfield established a farmer's market to provide fresh produce from the countryside. Local farmers rented stalls and sold their produce three days a week. Middle-class women began feeding their families through a daily round of "marketing." Eventually, only the working class continued to grow their own food, running swine in the streets and laboring after hours in what became the "poor man's garden."

Under the resulting ideology of Victorianism, named for the British queen who ascended the throne in 1837 (five years before the Lincolns married), men and women were said to inhabit "separate spheres." Men's sphere was the public world of work and politics, while women's sphere was the private world of home and family, where they toiled for the benefit of their husbands and children. Because women were not paid for their work, the work they performed was redefined as a duty, labeled the "domestic duty." The new ideology of separate spheres portrayed men and women as dramatically and indeed fundamentally different. Men were viewed as aggressive, competitive, and shrewd by nature, to compete in the new ruthless world of work. Women, by contrast, were considered gentle, loving, and sensitive creatures, best suited to nurture and succor their husbands and children. These gender differences were thought to complement each other and bind husband and wife together in a new "companionate" marriage, founded on emotional attachment. Industrialization therefore reshaped not only families themselves but also gender roles within families. The home became a refuge for middle-class men who expected their wives to keep house by day and then nurture them in the evening after they came home from work. Middle-class men and women were now conceived to be exact opposites so that both could perform their complementary roles within the family.

Newly emerging middle-class standards helped to shape private and public lives in Springfield. These newly genteel families strove to attain what was called "respectability" or "gentility," an aspiration not just to achieve wealth but to use their wealth to best advantage, displaying the cultural accoutrements and exhibiting the proper behaviors of polite society. Gentility was a social code signifying membership in an exclusive circle that transcended the workaday hubbub of the city and all the tribulations that bedeviled the "lower sort." Genteel Springfielders circulated in a world of soirees, calling cards, parlor games, and picnics that emulated the aristocratic culture of eastern cities. Above all, they strove to turn their homes into islands of tranquility amid the stormy sea of city life. The Lincoln home at Eighth and Jackson was tailor-made to serve just such a purpose. "Mary Todd came into Lincoln's life at one of its most important and critical periods," one of Lincoln's legal associates observed. "He needed far more than most men a refined and well-appointed home."

Starting life as the modest home of an Episcopal minister, the house gradually evolved into an exemplar of middle-class refinement. The clapboard house—less imposing than the brick residences of Aristocrat's Hill—appears white in the monochrome daguerreotypes of the day. In fact, it was a muted shade of brown, befitting the fashionable "brown decades" that preceded the later vogue for white that characterized the late nineteenth and early twentieth centuries. The picket fence, designed to keep both dogs and hogs at bay, set the home apart from the world around it. Lawns awaited the invention of garden hoses and lawn mowers, so yards of this period boasted shrubs and trees instead, symbolizing the taming of nature in the name of decorative display. The Lincolns welcomed the refinement that shrubs and trees exuded but spurned the labor they required, hiring nurserymen to do their planting instead. Lincoln's stepniece Harriet Chapman, who lived in the home during the 1840s, recalled that "I never knew him to make a garden, yet no one loved flowers better than he did." Middle-class men, and no one more than

Abraham Lincoln, renounced the tools that they had once wielded to till the land and typically left planting to their wives as part of their domestic management. As a local newspaper emphasized, "Most of our Ladies cultivate flowers." Springfield's Horticultural Society, organized in 1849, sponsored flower shows that encouraged women to develop and display their prowess at growing and arranging. Mary Lincoln never joined, and the family hired a Portuguese immigrant, Antonio Mendonsa, to tend their garden.

Climbing the front steps that elevated the house above the surrounding neighborhood, a visitor would pass through the rose bushes and enter the front hallway that protected the home from the world outside. Ideally, a servant would answer the door and announce the visitor by carrying a calling card up the stairs to the mistress of the house. The entryway typically contained a hat rack to receive coats and hats, an umbrella stand, and a table to greet the visitor with flowers and to receive calling cards. A mirror provided the visitor one last opportunity to groom, while a chair or bench afforded some comfort while the hosts composed themselves upstairs. Like most Victorian homes, the Lincoln house had two parlors, a front parlor to receive visitors and a back parlor to accommodate the family during their daily routine. Sliding doors or curtains separated the two parlors, denoting the boundary between public and private, which was one of the primary functions of the middle-class home. Comfort and conspicuous display demanded the finest furniture. The Lincolns' parlor featured walnut, mahogany, cherry, hickory, pine, and oak, along with a luxurious couch of horsehair, the most durable fabric of the age. Here, the couple received their neighbors during their endless rounds of "visiting" and entertained guests before and after the dinner parties that represented the middle-class housewife's proudest moments.

Indeed, Springfield's middle class enjoyed a steady rhythm of dinner parties. "There seems no bounds to the spirit of gayety and disipation just now," John Todd Stuart's wife Mary observed in 1855, "there has been one party and sometimes two or more, every evening for two weeks and a disposition still to keep it up." She moaned that "My list of acquaintances is becoming laboriously large. O, that I had strength to perform all my duties but it *is* pleasant after all to have a large circle of acquaintances." Still, these hostesses lived to entertain, and any lull in the social season readily produced an abject boredom. "The Legislature has adjourned," Mrs. Stuart reported in 1855. "Strangers all gone, and Springfield returned to its uniform dullness." A year later, she was still lamenting that "there is so little incident in my limited circle, I scarcely know what to write about."

Given Abraham Lincoln's profession and career ambitions, the Lincolns' social responsibilities were fundamentally political, yet they fell disproportionately on Mary. When the couple received an invitation to a "large entertainment" at the governor's house, she reported that "Mr L——*gives me* permission to go, but declines, the honor himself." In 1857, she described the disappointing turnout at one of her own parties. "About 500 hundred[*sic*] were invited," she wrote her half sister Emilie Todd Helm, "yet owing to an *unlucky* rain, 300 only favored us by their presence, and the same evening in Jacksonville Col Warren, gave a bridal party to his son." The swirling social scene was exhausting, however, especially for the hostess, and Mary reported with undoubted understatement a "slight fatigue." One summer she wrote a friend that "For the last two weeks, we have had a continual round of strawberry parties, this last week I have spent five evenings out—and you may suppose, that this day of rest, I am happy to enjoy." Looking forward to the social demands of New Year's Day, 1860, she wrote wearily that "it is quite late in the evening & tomorrow I must rise early, as it is *receiving* day."

In tune with their improving social situation, the Lincolns competed to entertain the city's loftiest social circles, and Mary Lincoln earned a reputation as a proficient hostess. "In her modest and simple home, everything orderly and refined, there was always, on the part of both host and hostess, a cordial and hearty Western welcome," one frequent guest noted. "Mrs. Lincoln's table was famed for the excellence of many rare Kentucky dishes, and in season, it was loaded with venison, wild turkeys, prairie chickens, quail and other game." Springfield's dinner parties were stunning not only in their number but also their dimensions. Mary Stuart, for example, reported with understatement that "we were invited, to a little family gathering at Dr Wallaces. When arrived we found the *family* extended, including some fifty or sixty. Quite a pleasant party it was." Even nine-year-old Willie's birthday "gala" in January 1860 attracted "50 or 60 boys & girls" into the Lincoln home, leading Mary to the forthright conclusion that "they are nonsensical affairs." Soon enough, she would find most of her time and attention, and indeed her historical reputation, devoted to such "nonsense" as First Lady.

Parenthood

Education, rather than land, represented the primary legacy of middle-class couples to their children. In between their ostentatious displays of hospitality, of course, middle-class women spent most of their lives keeping house and raising families. The new gender roles of the Victorian era consigned women to their homes to look after their children while their husbands braved the dangers of the city as providers for their families. Victorian culture elevated motherhood into an art and a science, indeed a solemn duty to raise morally upright sons and daughters.

In keeping with shifting patterns of middle-class child rearing, the size of families in Springfield fell dramatically while the Lincolns lived there. Limiting fertility allowed middle-class parents, and especially mothers, to devote more time, attention, and affection to each child as an individual, nurturing and educating their children to promote future success, rather than exacting immediate economic benefits, as Abraham Lincoln's parents had. One measure of fertility control is the "birth interval," the average period between childbirths. In Springfield, working-class women exhibited an interval between births of 2.7 years. Middle-class couples, by contrast, maintained a longer birth interval of 3.2 years, probably practicing some form of family limitation to allow them to devote more time and resources to fewer children.

In an era before artificial birth control, middle-class couples suppressed their fertility in a variety of ways. Typically, they began marrying later and delaying childbirth. By the 1840s, the decade during which the Lincolns married, women in Springfield had increased their marriage age by two years, which would suppress their fertility by one child, in most instances. Women also stopped bearing children earlier, thereby compressing their childbearing into a shorter span. Couples who married in Springfield bore all of their children during a period of nine years, on average, as compared to fourteen years among couples who had married earlier. After completing their families, women often retreated to a separate bedroom from their husbands to facilitate abstinence. If abstinence failed as a strategy for limiting childbearing, a variety of patent fertility suppressants was available to women in Springfield. Newspapers advertised "female pills" or "regulators" that came discreetly through the mail and cost as little as a dollar.

The Lincolns shared this emerging Victorian commitment to family limitation. Mary Lincoln, like most women, was acutely aware of the dangers of uncontrolled fertility. Her own mother, Eliza Todd, bore her children at a natural birth interval, every two years, but died from complications after her seventh childbirth, leaving Mary motherless at six. Her stepmother, Betsey, also observed a natural birth interval, bearing ten children in less than twenty years. Perhaps in response to the toll she witnessed in the Todd home, Mary Lincoln deferred her own marriage until age twenty-three, two years beyond the average age for brides in Springfield. She and Abraham Lincoln conceived their first son, Robert, within a month of their wedding but then began practicing some form of fertility limitation, achieving an overall birth interval of 3.2 years, which was perfectly average among Springfield's middle class (defined as practitioners of nonmanual occupations). Lincoln's frequent absences riding the circuit certainly facilitated abstinence, and after bearing their second son, Eddie, the couple waited almost five years before conceiving again. Eddie's death when he was almost four, however, prompted a third conception, which occurred almost immediately. One common strategy among parents who lost an infant was to bear another as quickly as possible to try to compensate, in part, for the loss. Willie, their third son, was born about eleven months after Eddie's death. Their fourth and final son, Tad, arrived just over two years later, conforming to a natural birth interval.

The Lincolns bore all of their children over a period of nine and one-half years, which was just about average for couples married in Springfield. Mary Lincoln completed her family at age thirty-five and devoted the rest of her married life to raising rather than bearing children, unlike her stepmother, who bore children well into her forties. Two years after Tad's birth, the Lincolns added a second bedroom, which was fashionable among prosperous Victorians. A second bedroom afforded privacy to wives who doted on grooming for their husbands while simultaneously facilitating abstinence. The arrangement likely indicated cooperation to attain middle-class respectability while limiting fertility, rather than signifying domestic discord. Mary Lincoln's family limitation likely had several motives. Both Abraham and Mary lost their mothers early in childhood and suffered emotionally at the hands of distant fathers, vying with stepsiblings for the attention of their fathers. Family limitation would have allowed them to dote on their children in an attempt to compensate, or even overcompensate, for their own turbulent childhoods. Career advancement was also a primary motive among middle-class parents, and the Lincolns may have agreed that they should devote as much time and energy to that goal as possible.

Presidential candidate Abraham Lincoln standing in front of the Lincolns' home at Eighth and Jackson Streets in Springfield with his sons Willie and Tad; photograph taken by John Adams Whipple in 1860. Library of Congress.

As fathers began leaving their homes to go to work, mothers bore an increasing share of child rearing duties, which burdened women such as Mary Lincoln with additional responsibilities. "Moral mothers" now shouldered the burden of shaping the character of their children as well as safeguarding their physical health and safety. A novel "intensive" motherhood demanded constant vigilance from mothers and instilled anxiety and fear for children's physical and spiritual well-being. Given her husband's long absences riding the Eighth Judicial Circuit, the primary responsibility for rearing their children fell to Mary Lincoln, which comported with the new Victorian definition of motherhood as crucial to the emotional nurture and character formation of their offspring. Like many middle-class mothers, Mary Lincoln was clearly an overprotective parent. Her children rarely left her sight, and when they did she overreacted. When Robert was three, for example, Abraham Lincoln wrote in a letter to Joshua Speed that "Since I began this letter a messenger came to tell me, Bob was lost; but by the time I reached the house, his mother had found him, and had him whip[p]ed—and, by now, very likely he is run away again." Many Victorian mothers practiced excessive moral and physical vigilance over their children. Fathers, on the other hand, were growing more distant from the management of children. Absent most of the time, like Lincoln, they increasingly overindulged their children when they had the opportunity.

In fairness to both Lincolns, they were trying to raise their sons during a period in which Victorians were redefining standards of both childhood and child rearing. Eddie's death from consumption was clearly a turning point in both their lives, driving home the vulnerability of their family while heightening their emotional commitment to their sons. Child mortality was an unfortunate fact of life in America until about 1880. In 1850, the year that Eddie Lincoln died, death claimed a staggering one in ten infants under the age of one in Springfield. Mortality in Eddie's age group, children under five, was considerably lower—3.5 percent—but still five times the rate of adult Springfielders. Tragically, one-fourth of all Springfielders who died during 1850 were infants under one, and one-half were children under five. The rate of death began leveling off at age five. Traditionally, child mortality bred an emotional distance between children and parents, who hesitated to make a psychological commitment until they were sure that their children would live. Until midcentury, parents tended to consider procreation, as well as infant death, an act of God over which they had no control. Victorian parents, however, especially mothers, were increasingly expected and even encouraged to grieve when they lost children. Just as conception was now viewed as voluntary, infant death began to seem preventable, heightening the sense of loss when a child did succumb. A family founded on affection rather than economic survival felt a heightened emotional emptiness upon losing any one of its members.

Losing Eddie reiterated the fragility of the Lincoln family even within their gated Victorian home and doubtlessly encouraged both parents to dote all the more on their two youngest children, Willie and Tad. Historians have speculated that the Lincolns' attitude toward rearing their first son, Robert, reflected their own barren relationships with imperious parents—Abraham's with his father, Thomas, and Mary's with her stepmother, Betsey. Both knew how to censure a child but neither knew how to nurture, and they therefore remained remote—and in Abraham Lincoln's instance frequently absent—during Robert's formative years. During the early years of their marriage, Robert took the brunt of their parental severity, and a servant remembered that "Ms L would whip Bob a great deal." Eddie's death at precisely midcentury coincided with a dramatic turning point in child rearing that placed emphasis on the malleability but essential purity of children's natures and encouraged parents to nurture them through reward rather than correct them through punishment. Now they gravitated to the opposite extreme of doting on their remaining sons' physical safety and emotional fulfillment, which became their fundamental concern and even obsession. As Mary observed of Abraham, "He was very very indulgent to his children—chided or praised for it he always said 'It is my pleasure that my children are free—happy and unrestrained by paternal tyranny. Love is the chain whereby to lock a child to its parent.'"

After little Eddie's death, both the Lincolns seem to have become even more permissive, and Willie and Tad virtually wallowed in their indulgence. Abraham Lincoln abetted and sometimes even joined them in the "pranks" they played on neighbors and visitors to the home. Victorian fathers generally engaged in play as a way of nurturing both their children and themselves. One acquaintance remembered Tad disrupting a meeting between his father and Lyman Trumbull, recalling that "the door opened and a boy dashed in, running as hard as he could. He was Tad." Rather than disciplining his son, Lincoln "stood up and opened wide his arms," and the visitors watched "both of them laughing and carrying on as if there was nobody looking at them." Lincoln freely admitted that "We never controlled our children much." When accused of whipping the boys, Mary Lincoln retorted that "if *I* have erred, it has been, in being too indulgent." Both of them tolerated innocent misbehavior, leading many acquaintances to detest the "brats," as Lincoln's law partner Herndon called them.

Mary soon developed a near-phobia about her children's health and safety. She grew to fear the world outdoors, in particular fretting over the intruders, dogs, and fires that continually plagued the city. During one of her husband's extended absences, neighbor James Gourley recalled, "She was crying & wailing one night—Called me and said—'Mr Gourly—Come—do Come & Stay with me all night—you Can Sleep in the bed with Bob and I.'" Sometimes she called out "Murder!" when confronted with a stranger or "Fire, Fire!" when fat caught flame on her stove. Another neighbor recalled that "one day I heard the scream—'Murder'—'Murder.' 'Murder'—turned round—Saw Mrs Lincoln up on the fence—hands up—Screaming—went to her—she said a big ferocious man had Entered her house—Saw an umbrella man come out—I suppose he had Entered to ask for old umbrellas to mend." When she summoned him to fend off a dog, he discovered "a little thing" that was "too small and good natured to do anything" yet managed to send Mary Lincoln into a panic. Her husband, too, could dote or even overreact. While he was in Congress, he wrote Mary that he had a "foolish dream about dear Bobby" that he could not forget until he heard that he was safe. When Robert suffered an all-too-real dog bite, Lincoln took him the 140 miles to Terre Haute, Indiana, where a "mad stone" reputedly had the power to prevent rabies. In the parents' defense, it must be said that Springfield was indeed a dangerous city. Intruders, fire, and dogs took their toll every day, as did the specter of infant death that stalked the streets in the form of infectious disease. The Lincolns doted on their children literally to keep them alive, all the more in the wake of their inability to prevent little Eddie's death. Shortly before the family left for Washington, Mary's younger sister, Ann, lost her ten-year-old son to typhoid fever. "The family are almost inconsolable," Mary observed with compassion, "& for the last week, I have spent the greater portion of my time, with them." Such a loss could only have driven home the fragility of her own children's health, and she understandably avowed that "I trust never to witness *such suffering ever* again."

Turmoil

Less tangibly, however, the Lincolns' transition to Victorianism remained incomplete. The couple often violated the very middle-class expectations that lay at the foundation of their marriage. Put simply, the new, middle-class values set a nearly impossible standard that all too often the Lincolns failed to meet. For a variety of reasons, both members of the couple fell short of middle-class conventions. Despite its growing cultural potency, as an emerging ethic of family life in America, Victorianism remained untested and ambiguous. Newly married couples were unfamiliar with its demanding dictates, especially for women, its arcane domestic duties, and its exacting gender roles. For this reason, a flood of advice literature, including etiquette books for women and success manuals for men, emerged to prepare wives and husbands for the challenging gender roles they must now obey. On New Year's Eve, 1846, for example, Abraham Lincoln stopped at a general store in Springfield and bought Mary two domestic manuals, "Miss Leslie's Housekeeper" and "Miss Leslie's Cookery." The timing suggests an attempt to improve his wife's housekeeping skills as part of a New Year's resolution. (Whether Abraham presented the books as a gift or bought them at Mary's direction is an intriguing but moot question.) Further, middle-class marriages were a decided minority. By 1860, the middle class included no more than one-tenth of Illinois families and only one-fourth of families in Springfield. Far too often, middle-class status was precarious or even fleeting. Between 1850 and 1860, three out of ten middle-class families in Springfield actually fell in status and slipped back into the ranks of the working class. In short, maintaining a middle-class marriage, even in Springfield, could be problematic.

Above all, Abraham and Mary Lincoln approached their middle-class marriage from two opposing cultural perspectives. When he married, Abraham Lincoln was just leaving the traditional, folk economy in which he had grown up. He found himself *rising* into the new middle class in Springfield, making a definite leap upward. When she married, by contrast, Mary Lincoln *fell* from her perch within the comfortable upper class of the Lexington Bluegrass, taking a definite step downward into Springfield's middle class. "Mrs. Lincoln came from the best of stock, and was raised like a lady," according to one of her relatives. "Her husband was her opposite, in origins, in education, in breeding, in everything." The middle class therefore posed a social and cultural gulf that separated the Lincolns from other families and from one another. Both Lincolns strove to lead a respectable middle-class marriage, which was, after all, the ideal for Americans of their age. Yet Abraham Lincoln continually reverted to the traditional patterns of family life in which he had been raised, while Mary Lincoln continually attempted to reproduce the upper-class lifestyle that she found so familiar. Instead of a middle ground uniting this couple from such disparate backgrounds, the middle class too often became a battleground, because neither partner ever successfully fulfilled the exacting strictures of the new middle class. Above all, Abraham Lincoln's vocation—law—and his avocation—politics—continually blurred the boundaries between public and private that were so central to the new middle-class existence.

As a wife, Mary Lincoln's foremost duty was to keep a home for her husband. "At home he had at all times the watchful and efficient attention of Mrs. Lincoln to every detail of his daily life as regards those things she had learned were most essential to keep him at his constitutional best," wrote a lawyer who knew Lincoln. "Mrs. Lincoln, by her attention, had much to do with preserving her husband's health. She was careful to see that he ate his meals regularly, and that he was well groomed. He was not naturally inclined to give much thought to his clothes, and if Mrs. Lincoln happened to be away from Springfield for a few days on a trip out of the city, we were pretty sure to be apprised of her absence by some slight disorder in Lincoln's apparel and his irregularity at meal-time." This positive contribution, however, could easily acquire a negative tone, as when an acquaintance heard Mary snap, "Why don't you dress up and try to look like somebody?" In short, middle-class status *empowered* Mary Lincoln but also *burdened* her with constant and nearly complete supervision of the Lincoln family. Further, her feminine authority ended at the front door at Eighth and Jackson. Abraham Lincoln enjoyed tremendous prestige within the public sphere that diminished the moment he stepped inside his own home. Mary Lincoln, by contrast, enjoyed a profound domestic authority that dissolved the moment she stepped outside her own front door.

To his credit, Abraham Lincoln understood, without fully embracing, this middle-class separation of spheres. Like other ambitious middle-class men, he often felt more at ease in his office than in his own home. A colleague noticed that "Lincoln, when in this little office, was more easy in manner and unrestrained in all respects than at any other place I ever saw him." Away from home, Abraham Lincoln enjoyed a spontaneous and varied social life: "He would leave to call at Diller's drug-store, or at one of the dry-goods stores, to meet a friendly group in the counting-room, or more often to meet friends at the State House, that was directly across the street from his law office, to visit the offices there, or spent an hour or two in the State Library." Like many men of his era, Lincoln clearly valued this public sphere, to which men alone had access, over the private one. He once conceded that "I myself manage all important matters. In little things I have got along through life by letting my wife run her end of the machine pretty much in her own way." This is a succinct, indeed shrewd, assessment of the newly emerging gender roles. Still, Lincoln's "little things" were the family's domestic affairs, while his "important matters" took place outside the home, in the masculine world of work and politics.

All too often, Abraham Lincoln violated the new Victorian standards. As his law partner, William Herndon, acknowledged, "Such want of social polish on the part of her husband of course gave Mrs. Lincoln great offence." Mary's role as wife was to enforce the very standards that her husband so frequently transgressed. "It is therefore quite natural that she should complain if he answered the door-bell himself instead of sending the servant to do so," one of her relatives explained, "neither is she to be condemned if, as you say, she raised 'merry war' because he persisted in using his own knife in the butter, instead of the silver-handled one intended for that purpose." Lincoln was acutely aware of his own lack of polish and avoided awkward social situations. According to Herndon, "For fashionable society he had a marked dislike, although he appreciated its value in promoting the welfare of a man ambitious to succeed in politics." In short, Lincoln understood and valued middle-class mores but never mastered them. Indeed this "consciousness of his shortcomings as a society man rendered him unusually diffident." He often cloaked his own awkwardness with a whimsical humor that seemed like indifference. On one occasion, for example, Lincoln answered the front door in his shirtsleeves and admitted two women, "notifying them in his open familiar way, that he would 'trot the women folks out.'" Mary's anger, of course, was "instantaneous." Yet Lincoln seemed to enjoy flaunting the genteel values that Mary cherished but that he could never master. After he became president, for example, Mary once caught Abraham feeding a cat with a gold fork at a dinner party. In response, Lincoln reasoned that "If the gold fork was good enough for Buchanan I think it is good enough for Tabby."

When his humor failed him, Lincoln's best recourse was to retreat, which the new separation of spheres actually facilitated. During social occasions at home, Lincoln drew on gender roles as a shield against unwonted gentility. As Herndon related, "at the very first opportunity he would have the men separated from their ladies and crowded close around him in one corner of the parlor," much to Mary's disgust. Quite often, he would simply leave home. Contemporaries attributed his long absences to Mary. When a domestic spat loomed, a neighbor recalled, Abraham would "suddenly think of an engagement he had downtown, grasp his hat, and start for his office." During their worst episodes, Lincoln might go to work early and come home late or never go home at all. His profession, of course, abetted these absences, as when he spent weeks on end riding the circuit. In this fashion, Lincoln could turn the Victorian separation of spheres to his own advantage. Christopher Lasch has argued that the middle class viewed the home as a "haven in a heartless world." Lincoln, like many men, inverted this formula, seeking refuge away from home in the masculine public world, turning to work as a "haven from a heartless home." As Herndon put it bluntly, "his home was *Hell*" and "absence from home was his *Heaven*." Still others put a positive face on his long absences. "The fact that Mary Todd, by her turbulent nature and unfortunate manner, prevented her husband from becoming a domestic man, operated largely in his favor," one sympathetic friend reminisced; "for he was thereby kept out in the world of business and politics."

And yet Mary Lincoln, too, violated middle-class standards in her attempts to reproduce the upper-class surroundings of her youth. Herndon considered her "cold & repulsive to visitors that did not suit her cold aristocratic blood," and a neighbor agreed that she "put on plenty style." Like many middle-class housewives, Mary Lincoln had trouble finding, managing, and keeping servants. In fact, according to a neighbor, she "was quite disposed to make a servant girl of her husband." Lincoln would "get the breakfast and then dress the children" and finally "wash the dishes before going to his office," a pointed violation of Victorian gender roles. While performing routine housework, Mary once asked rhetorically, "What would my poor father say if he found me doing this kind of work." While attempting to live beyond her means, she still provoked charges of stinginess, confronting the perpetual dilemma of the middle-class housewife—making her home comfortable for her husband while advancing his career, all on a middle-class budget.

The semi-public life of a politician (not to mention a president) challenged many of the basic premises on which Victorian marriages rested. Above all, political life blurred the line between public and private that lay at the heart of family life. The overall divorce rate in Springfield was very low, just 1.3 percent, between 1850 and 1860. But divorce rates varied dramatically among the city's occupational groups, three of which—farmers, merchants, and professionals—enjoyed extremely stable marriages during the decade. Not a single household head who engaged in agriculture, commerce, or a profession divorced between 1850 and 1860. Surprisingly, class differences were irrelevant. Both middle-class and working-class couples experienced a thoroughly average divorce rate during the decade—1.3 percent. At the other extreme, however, one occupational group—public officials—stood out. Officeholders exhibited far and away the highest divorce rate in Springfield. During the 1850s, almost 9 percent of officeholders divorced, a stunning seven times the average. In fact, couples that Abraham Lincoln knew experienced a divorce rate three times higher than those he didn't know. Clearly, involvement in politics and public service put unusual stresses upon otherwise typical marriages. By blurring the line between public and private life, politics, it seems, bred stormy marriages.

Politics

Throughout his four terms in the state legislature, Lincoln was a leading advocate of the Whig philosophy of improvement and in particular the economic program of his idol Henry Clay—government-funded transportation, a national bank to provide a stable currency, and a protective tariff to stimulate economic growth. During his first term, Lincoln supported the creation of the State Bank of Illinois, headquartered in Springfield with branches in eight other towns. He sponsored transportation improvements in Sangamon County, including the construction of state roads running to Springfield. Dreaming of a water route linking Springfield and the Illinois River, he pushed for a canal running along the Sangamon River, which was approved but never built. More grandly, Lincoln supported construction of the Illinois and Michigan Canal and the Illinois Central Railroad. In 1836, he was reelected to the legislature as part of the "Long Nine" who represented Sangamon County. Eight of the nine were Whigs, and they all supported an ambitious scheme of internal improvements, including a network of publicly financed canals and railroads, which won approval. Lincoln also played a key role in moving the state capital from Vandalia to Springfield, ensuring the economic growth and political importance of central Illinois.

While growing up, practicing law, and serving in government, Lincoln developed an eloquent commitment to human equality and acquired a passionate belief in the moral injustice of slavery. His earliest experiences with slavery occurred long before he came to Illinois. He had little contact with slaves and slave-owners as a boy in Hardin County, Kentucky, which boasted mostly free, white family farmers rather than large slave plantations. About one-eighth of the county's population were slaves. By contrast, slaves comprised fully one-third of the population of Mary Todd's childhood home of Fayette County, Kentucky. Abraham Lincoln similarly had little experience with free African Americans as a boy. Only 3 percent of Hardin County's African Americans, twenty-eight of them, were free. Moving to Indiana isolated Lincoln even further from African Americans, both slave and free. In Spencer County, where in his own words he "grew up," there were no slaves and only fourteen African Americans. His first memorable glimpses of slavery occurred on his two voyages down the Mississippi River to New Orleans. His earliest recorded racial memory originated during his first trip down the river with Allen Gentry when he was nineteen. Thirty years later, Lincoln remembered that "one night they were attacked by seven negroes with intent to kill and rob them." During his second trip southward, guiding Denton Offutt's flatboat in 1831, Lincoln caught a glimpse of a slave market in New Orleans that his cousin John Hanks believed made an indelible mark and moved him to sympathize with African American slaves. "There it was we Saw Negroes Chained—maltreated—whipt & scourged," Hanks recalled. "I can say Knowingly that it was on this trip that he formed his opinions of Slavery: it ran its iron in him then & there." By his own account, Lincoln's early experiences as a youth helped to shape the racial views of the man. "I am naturally anti-slavery," he reflected as president. "If slavery is not wrong, nothing is wrong. I can not remember when I did not so think and feel."

When Lincoln settled in New Salem, there were 38 African Americans in Sangamon County out of a total population of more than

12,000. While most of them (just over two-thirds) were free, in the entire county, only one African American, Lucy Roundtree, headed an independent household. Every other African American was a servant living within a white family. Six residents of the county, including John Todd, the patriarch of the Springfield Todds, owned slaves. Todd, in fact, owned four slaves, two boys and two girls, making him the largest slave-owner in the county. Despite the Northwest Ordinance's prohibition of slavery, local government accommodated slave-owners by allowing them to "register" servants and "apprentice" African American children, whom they could literally buy and sell like slaves. In 1835, for example, John Todd took on an eight-year-old African American girl as an unpaid apprentice "to learn the art and mystery of domestic housewifery" until she turned eighteen. In 1835, Ninian Edwards took on an eleven-year-old African American orphan girl to practice "domestic housewifery" in his household until 1842. In short, Abraham Lincoln courted Mary Todd in a home that included an African American slave.

The year before Abraham Lincoln married Mary Todd, he had an experience with slavery that profoundly affected his view of the institution and of African Americans and, indeed, haunted his thoughts on the subject for the rest of his life. In 1841, he visited his old friend Joshua Speed near Louisville, Kentucky. Speed had recently inherited an opulent plantation, Farmington, along with its more than seventy slaves. After two months, Lincoln and Speed returned together to Illinois, riding a riverboat down the Ohio to St. Louis, where they boarded a stagecoach for Springfield. On the riverboat, Lincoln witnessed the eerie spectacle of a dozen slaves coffered together, as he put it, "like so many fish upon a trot-line," an experience that haunted him forever. "In this condition they were being separated forever from the scenes of their childhood, their friends, their fathers and mothers, and brothers and sisters, and many of them, from their wives and children," he reflected with an eloquence on the subject that would soon become second nature, "and going into perpetual slavery where the lash of the master is proverbially more ruthless and unrelenting than any other where." He called this memory "a continual torment to me." Significantly, however, he condemned the slave trade that destroyed these families and sent slaves westward but not the slavery on a plantation like Farmington. Just as tellingly, he sympathized with the slaves but firmly believed that he personally could do nothing to ameliorate their plight.

The Lincolns' personal relations with free African Americans in Springfield were always respectful, yet they interacted with them only as servants. At least four African Americans worked as domestic servants for the Lincolns. Ruth Stanton, known as "Aunt Ruth," Jane Jenkins, who lived a block away, and Mariah Vance, who served as cook and nursemaid for the boys during the 1850s, worked for Mary Lincoln. At the time of his election as president, Lincoln employed an African American driver and valet, William H. Johnson. He took Johnson to Washington on the family's two-week railway journey as his personal servant and on his trip to Gettysburg. Among all the African Americans in Springfield, Lincoln developed his closest relationship with his barber, William Florville. A native Haitian of French ancestry, Florville was a so-called "creole" and the only foreign-born African American in Springfield. His barber shop thrived, and he expanded his business to include the first laundry in the city. He began buying property on Lincoln's advice and grew wealthy, becoming the community's most prosperous African American. An active leader in the African American community, he contributed to charities and churches and headed the movement to found an African American school.

As a young legislator, Lincoln reflected traditional racial views in opposing equal rights for African Americans. During his first two terms, for example, he voted to continue restricting the elective franchise to whites. In fact, he never publicly advocated the extension of political rights to African Americans until a few days before his death. However, Lincoln was also far ahead of his time in insisting that slavery was an injustice that must be eradicated and that all people, black as well as white, had the same right to share in the kinds of opportunities for self-improvement that he and all other free Americans enjoyed. He believed that slavery not only exploited African Americans but blighted American society in general by limiting the nation's potential to develop socially and economically. In

1837, a month before leaving New Salem, Lincoln took his first public stand against slavery when he and a legislative colleague, Dan Stone, declared that "They believe that the institution of slavery is founded on both injustice and bad policy" and called for the abolition of slavery in the District of Columbia. This was a remarkable stand for a twenty-eight-year-old legislator from New Salem, Illinois, to take, and it culminated a quarter-century later when President Lincoln signed both the Emancipation Proclamation and an act of Congress abolishing slavery in the District of Columbia. Fundamentally, Lincoln believed that ending slavery not only guaranteed freedom and opportunity for all Americans but was also essential in promoting the nation's social and economic development.

After four terms in the Illinois legislature, Lincoln retired briefly from politics to focus on building a respectable legal career that could help him support his growing family. All the while, he continued to play a prominent role in Whig political circles, campaigning for other candidates and serving as a presidential elector. In 1844, he stumped extensively for Whig presidential nominee Henry Clay in that losing effort. By 1846, his years of party service, political organizing, and personal campaigning paid off in his nomination for Congress. Anticlimactically, the Springfield newspaper, the *Sangamo Journal*, noted that "This nomination was of course anticipated—there being no other candidate in the field." Lincoln's clearest rival was John J. Hardin, a former congressman and Mary Todd's third cousin. Hardin accepted his defeat at Lincoln's hands graciously and conceded that "It is Abraham['s] turn now." In 1846, the Seventh Congressional District virtually belonged to the Whigs. Considered a "safe seat," it was the only Whig district in the state of Illinois. Whigs first captured the seat in 1838 and held it through five consecutive terms of Congress. Lincoln was confident of victory and indeed won 56 percent of the vote, the largest landslide in the history of the district. Still, the young politician who ever aspired to still greater things soon wrote that "Being elected to Congress, though I am very grateful to our friends, for having done it, has not pleased me as much as I expected."

In October 1847, the Lincolns left Springfield for Washington. "Mr. Lincoln, the member of Congress elect from this district, has just set out on his way to the city of Washington," the local news-paper reported by way of a farewell. "His family is with him; they intend to visit their friends and relatives in Kentucky before they take up the line of march for the seat of government. Success to our talented member of Congress! He will find many men in Congress who possess twice the good looks, and not half the good sense, of our own representative." The family visited the Todds for three weeks in Lexington, Kentucky, on their way to Washington. After growing accustomed to their spacious Springfield home, the Lincolns now returned to boarding in Washington. They moved into Mrs. Sprigg's boardinghouse, a short walk from the Capitol (on the present site of the Library of Congress). Known as a Whig establishment, Mrs. Sprigg's had hosted Lincoln's predecessors in Congress, John Todd Stuart and Edward Baker, after whom little Eddie had been named. Mary Lincoln was disappointed to discover that she was the only congressional wife in residence at Mrs Sprigg's. As she had in the Globe Tavern, she landed unwittingly in yet another male enclave.

The Washington winter found the four Lincolns confined uncom-fortably to a single room. When spring arrived, Mary Lincoln gath-ered the two children and returned to her family in Lexington. At age thirty-nine, for the first and only time in his entire life, Abraham Lincoln had to live alone. Accustomed to sharing camaraderie and even a bed with his male roommates, not to mention his wife Mary, Lincoln abhorred this self-imposed solitude. In a poignant tribute to the couple's affections, he wrote Mary that "In this troublesome world, we are never quite satisfied. When you were here, I thought you hindered me some in attending to business; but now, having nothing but business—no variety—it has grown exceedingly tasteless to me." Expressing characteristic tenderness for his sons, Lincoln told Mary, "Dont let the blessed fellows forget father." Mary wrote a long letter assuring him "How much, I wish instead of writing, *we* were together this evening, I feel very sad away from you." In concluding, she enjoined him, "Do not fear the children, have forgotten you."

Lincoln's single term in Congress was dominated by the Mexi-can War and the looming sectional crisis over slavery. As the only Whig congressman from Illinois, Lincoln felt obligated to represent the views of the party that he had helped to build. Illinois Whigs insisted that they did not oppose the war itself but only the suspicious circumstances under which it began. "Mr. Polk's War," as they labeled it, seemed an attempt to enhance southern political power by adding new slave territory to the Union. Illinois Whigs supported the war once it was underway but wanted a speedy conclusion. Lincoln now set out to make a major statement in opposition to Polk's handling of the war by introducing his famous "Spot Resolutions." The resolutions focused on the origins of the war and particularly Polk's insistence that Mexico "invaded our territory, and shed the blood of our fellow citizens on our own soil." Lincoln asked Polk whether the "spot" on which the war began was truly American soil or the just possession of Mexico. The implication was that Polk had provoked an unnecessary war with territorial acquisition as its goal, not national security or honor.

As a moderate, however, Lincoln continued the stance that he had taken while in the Illinois legislature—that slavery was wrong, indeed evil, but that Congress had no power to interfere with it in southern states. Instead, he concentrated on attacking slavery only where Congress had undisputed authority to end it, in the western territories and the District of Columbia. Lincoln therefore supported the Wilmot Proviso, designed to exclude slavery from any new territory acquired from Mexico. He declared proudly that he voted for it at least forty times. He also promoted an amendment abolishing slavery in the nation's capital. Neither measure won passage. Lincoln's stance marked him as a moderate who would not confront slavery directly but would do everything possible to prevent its spread. During his single congressional term, Lincoln witnessed the creation of a new and powerful antislavery crusade, the Free-Soil movement, dedicated to attacking slavery indirectly by prohibiting it not in the South but wherever Congress had a clear power to end it—in the western territories.

Always a practitioner of the politically possible, Lincoln endorsed Zachary Taylor for president, largely because he believed that Henry Clay had no chance to win the election. "In my judgment," he reasoned, "we can elect nobody but Gen; Taylor." Lincoln attended the Whig national convention in Philadelphia to witness Taylor's nomination and embarked on a speaking tour of the Northeast on Taylor's behalf. Privately, Lincoln was already a supporter of what he called "nonextension," opposition to the westward spread of slavery. During his campaign for Congress, he explained to an abolitionist that while he was opposed to slavery, he felt legally bound to tolerate it in the South, where it already existed. He was committed, however, to preventing its spread into new territories. "I hold it to be a para-mount duty of us in the free states, due to the Union of the states, and perhaps to liberty itself (paradox though it may seem) to let the slavery of the other states alone," he concluded, "while, on the other hand, I hold it to be equally clear, that we should never knowingly lend ourselves directly or indirectly, to prevent that slavery from dying a natural death—to find new places for it to live in, when it can no longer exist in the old." Lincoln, in short, believed in free soil but not abolitionism. He was committed to preventing the spread of slavery but was not willing to attack it where it already existed. He would oppose any antislavery party simply because it had no chance of winning an election and would ironically help elect a Democrat by dividing the Whigs. "By the *fruit* the tree is to be known," he concluded. Only the Whig Party could "bring forth *good* fruit" by preventing the spread of slavery into the territories.

Over the summer, Mary Lincoln decided to reunite the family by bringing the two boys back to Mrs. Sprigg's in Washington. Although he welcomed his family, Lincoln worried about potential distractions, as well as Mary's ability to get along with the other boarders. "Will you be a *good girl* in all things, if I consent?" he queried. "Then come along, and that as *soon* as possible." Before they arrived, he received bills from two shops in Washington that he knew nothing about. "I hesitated to pay them," he wrote Mary, "because my recollection is that you told me when you went away, there was nothing left unpaid." He surely had no reason to suspect that the future held out many more such occurrences that would someday become a familiar way of life for his wife Mary.

As Lincoln's sojourn in Washington reiterated, Mary Lincoln proved a significant asset to her husband's political ambitions but could also unthinkingly complicate his public life. Raised in a family of politicians who encouraged her to speak her mind, she never hesitated to engage in electioneering, which she herself characterized as "rather an unladylike profession." Immersing herself in William Henry Harrison's "Log Cabin Campaign" of 1840, for example, she reasoned that "at such a *crisis*, whose heart could remain untouched"—whether male or female? Lincoln never failed to bristle at the suggestion that his marriage had any political motivations, but after all politics had drawn the two of them together in the first place. Lincoln's Todd in-laws were reliable political allies early in his career, until the sectional crisis pulled some of them, including Ninian Edwards and John Todd Stuart, into the Democratic Party. Mary Lincoln's social graces as a hostess were also politically helpful, as were her alliances with the wives of her husband's associates, including Julia Trumbull, Adeline Judd, Mary Brayman, Mercy Conkling, Mary Stuart, and Eliza Browning. In fact, few of Mary's confidantes were not political wives—or "widows." Her early friends Mercy Levering and Julia Jayne married Whig leaders—James Conkling and Lyman Trumbull, respectively—as did two of her sisters.

Mary believed that her chief political skill was in judging the character of her husband's allies and potential appointees. A year after his assassination, she told William Herndon that "My husband placed great Confidence in my knowledge in human nature; he had not much knowledge of men." She may have meant that her husband was too charitable toward political associates and subordinates. She herself was unwilling or unable to forgive. Her belief in her superior ability to judge encouraged her to meddle, mostly in appointments and dismissals rather than formal policy formation, and hence to make enemies, sometimes out of friends. After Lyman Trumbull defeated Lincoln for a U.S. Senate seat, for example, Mary resolved never to speak to her closest friend, Julia Jayne Trumbull, again. She kept her vow. As her husband's rise to national prominence produced political rivals, Mary Lincoln expressed her unconditional loyalty by banishing most of her Springfield friends from her social circle, one by one.

After returning from Washington, Lincoln virtually retired from politics. He later wrote that "I was losing interest in politics, when the repeal of the Missouri Compromise aroused me again." In January 1854, Senator Stephen Douglas, Democrat of Illinois, introduced the Kansas-Nebraska Bill, repealing the Missouri Compromise and allowing popular sovereignty to decide the question of slavery in the Kansas and Nebraska Territories. In May, Congress passed the Kansas-Nebraska Act, reintroducing slavery into a region that had been guaranteed to remain free since 1820 and therefore violated the principle of nonextension. A coalition of Whigs, Free-Soilers, and Anti-Nebraska Democrats gradually arose in Illinois to oppose the Kansas-Nebraska Act. Lincoln initially clung to the Whig Party as the best hope for defeating the Democrats and overturning the act. He also avoided the Anti-Nebraska coalition because it included nativists, anti-Catholics, and prohibitionists as well as nonextensionists. In particular, Lincoln refused to cooperate with Know Nothings, members of the nativist American Party. In the fall of 1854, Lincoln delivered a series of speeches emphasizing the immorality of slavery, labeling it a "monstrous injustice" and declaring that "I hate it." Yet he reiterated his aversion for abolitionism and his support for nonextension as the best approach to ending slavery. In early 1856, Lincoln framed a statement of principles that united the Anti-Nebraska coalition behind his antislavery doctrine and paved the way for the emergence of the Republican Party in Illinois. During the presidential election of 1856, he served as an elector for the Republican nominee, John C. Frémont, and campaigned vigorously on his behalf. Illinois went for the Democratic candidate, James Buchanan, but Republicans were proud to have elected a senator and a governor, neither of which a generation of Whigs had been able to do.

In the wake of the U.S. Supreme Court's *Dred Scott* decision of 1857, which denied citizenship to African Americans, Lincoln elaborated his views on slavery to emphasize legal equality as a natural right that was guaranteed by the Declaration of Independence. In 1858, Illinois Republicans nominated Lincoln to compete for Stephen Douglas's U.S. Senate seat. Lincoln and Douglas conducted seven debates across the state. Throughout the campaign, Lincoln reiterated that slavery was wrong, a "great moral, social, and political evil." The debates won him praise as an eloquent but pragmatic opponent of slavery and gained him a wider following throughout the North. Republicans won the popular vote, but the state's apportionment system favored the Democrats. Douglas's reelection to the Senate proved a temporary victory, because his support for popular sovereignty and opposition to the *Dred Scott* decision alienated Democrats in the Deep South, who now considered him unacceptable as a presidential nominee.

Abraham Lincoln during his presidential campaign, at age fifty-one; photograph taken by Preston Butler on August 13, 1860. Library of Congress.

In 1860, four major parties proposed solutions to the slavery issue. Northern Democrats nominated Douglas for president and advocated popular sovereignty in western territories. Southern Democrats nominated John C. Breckinridge of Kentucky, Buchanan's vice president and a defender of slavery expansion, demanding federal protection of slavery in the West. The Constitutional Union Party rallied former Whigs in the Upper South. They supported the Union, advocated a constitutional compromise over slavery, and nominated John Bell of Tennessee. Meeting in Chicago, Republicans nominated Lincoln as a moderate who would recognize southern states' right to retain slavery but would strictly enforce nonextension through the Free-Soil doctrine.

Lincoln won 59 percent of the electoral votes, all from the North, but a popular plurality of less than 40 percent, the smallest winning percentage of any president in American history. Bell won Virginia, Kentucky, and Tennessee; Douglas, only one state, Missouri; and Breckinridge every other slave state. After the election, seven states in the Deep South, believing that Lincoln's nonextension policy would ultimately destroy slavery, seceded from the Union, began seizing federal forts and arsenals, and created the Confederate States of America.

THE PRESIDENT AND THE FIRST LADY

Washington

In February 1861, the Lincoln family made a twelve-day railway journey to Washington that represented a turning point not only in their lives but in the fate of the nation as well. The traveling party numbered all five Lincolns, including Robert, who was now a student at Harvard College, as well as Lincoln's newly appointed secretaries, John Nicolay and John Hay, brother-in-law and family doctor William Wallace, and a young law clerk, Elmer Ellsworth, who was raising a company of dashing Zouaves to help prepare the Union for the worst. Half a dozen Illinois politicians boarded the train to advise the president-elect. Ward Hill Lamon, a longtime legal colleague and friend, acted as Lincoln's personal bodyguard, but the army provided a colonel, a major, and a captain as a sort of military escort. William H. Johnson, Lincoln's African American valet, attended the president-elect throughout the journey. The caravan visited the capitals of five states (Indiana, Ohio, New York, Pennsylvania, and New Jersey) and many of the largest cities in the North, including New York and Philadelphia. The goal was to introduce the largely unknown Lincoln to the nation and rally support for the now beleaguered Union. Mary Lincoln initiated her new role as First Lady by hosting a succession of receptions in the larger cities, whenever time permitted.

In the wake of Abraham Lincoln's election as president, the federal government's hold on Washington was so precarious that many of his supporters feared he would never reach the city. With disloyalty rampant, assassination plots brewing, and coup attempts in the off-ing, Lincoln's friends persuaded him to enter Washington by night, wearing a disguise, to lay his claim to the contested presidency. He later confided to Ward Hill Lamon, now the marshal of the District of Columbia, that "the way we skulked into this city, in the first place, has been a source of shame and regret to me, for it did look so cowardly!" He quickly went on the offensive to secure Washington, transform it into a base of military operations against the Confederacy, make it a symbol of a resilient and enduring Union, and, in short, turn it into a truly national capital. (He later called this task "cleaning the devil out of Washington.") He arrested the mayor for disloyalty, declared martial law to keep the railroad and telegraph running to Baltimore, and authorized construction of a ring of forts to defend the city. Situated in the midst of the Eastern Theatre of war and sandwiched between two slave states, Washington held tremendous strategic, political, and moral significance for both the Union and the Confederacy. Surrounded by Confederate armies in Virginia and southern sympathizers in Maryland and lying just one hundred miles from the Confederate capital, Richmond, Civil War Washington was a beleaguered and often insecure island of nationalism amid a seeming sea of disunion.

Strategically, Washington was the greatest military target and potential prize for Confederate armies, just as capturing Richmond remained the Union's primary military goal throughout the war. From the First Battle of Bull Run onward, Confederate armies con-tinually threatened Washington as part of General Robert E. Lee's strategy of "taking the war to the enemy." Lee's summer offensives of 1862 and 1863, which culminated in the turning points of Antietam and Gettysburg, were primarily designed to threaten Washington, encourage southern sympathizers in the North, and challenge the Lincoln administration's authority to govern. At Lee's behest, Stone-wall Jackson's army could emerge from the Shenandoah Valley and advance on Washington whenever the Army of the Potomac neared Richmond. As a result, President Lincoln insisted on maintaining an army of 15,000 to 50,000 men around the capital, which denied needed manpower to the Union offensives. (Lincoln explained simply that "I must have troops to defend this Capital.") During the winter of 1861–62, after the Union's unexpected defeat in the First Battle of Bull Run, Congress authorized the construction of a thirty-seven-mile-long ring of fortifications around Washington. The defensive system eventually included sixty-eight forts connected by twenty miles of trenches. Ninety-three artillery positions in the fortified ring boasted 800 cannons. Indeed, by the end of the war, Washington was the most heavily defended city on earth. Yet during the summer of 1864, Confederate general Jubal Early led a raid on the city that tested its defenses and by turns panicked and rallied its residents, including President Lincoln, who rushed to Fort Stevens to witness the repulse of the enemy army. Within these barricades sat a city of 63,000 people, America's twelfth largest in 1860. With its ebb and flow of armies, its sprawling defenses, and its overflowing hospitals, hotels, theaters, and prisons, Washington's population more than tripled in size during the war, swelling at times to 200,000. Union armies, composed of volunteers and draftees from across the North, moved continually through the city, up to 140,000 at a time. Newspaper correspondents from across the United States and Europe, foreign dignitaries and military observers from around the world, and tourists by the thousands crammed the hotels and sought entertainment in the theaters, music halls, saloons, and gambling dens that proliferated during the war. Confederate deserters, opportunists of all varieties, including war profiteers, spiritualists, and prostitutes, as well as clandestine rings of southern spies and assassins, abounded.

Above all, the city filled up with wounded soldiers in the wake of every major military engagement in the Eastern Theatre. At the beginning of the war, makeshift hospitals ministered to the wounded and sick, more than 56,000 soldiers during the first year alone. Midway through the war, more sanitary open-air, or "pavilion," hospitals—about thirty of them—each with ten or twelve wards housing 600 patients, dotted the city. Volunteers from across the North, including Clara Barton, Louisa May Alcott, and Walt Whitman, spent their days tending to the wounded. Whitman alone ministered to approximately 100,000 wounded men, northerners and southerners alike. President Lincoln and his wife Mary visited the hospitals frequently, extending both personal and symbolic comfort to the wounded. Abraham Lincoln, for example, spent part of July 4, 1862, riding with a train of ambulances carrying wounded soldiers from the Peninsular Campaign to a makeshift hospital at the Soldiers' Home and two years later visited three hospitals and shook hands with a thousand wounded soldiers in a single day. Convalescent soldiers and their families often visited the Lincolns at the White House, to receive their thanks and to inspire them in return. When the "One-Legged Brigade" from St. Elizabeth's Hospital assembled outside the White House, Abraham Lincoln called them "orators," whose very appearance spoke louder than any words. The day before he left for Gettysburg, Lincoln reviewed 2,500 members of the Invalid Corps as they marched en masse down Pennsylvania Avenue past the White House. Mary Lincoln not only visited the wounded but raised funds to help support the hospitals do their work. On December 23, 1863, she served Christmas dinners to wounded soldiers in area hospitals. The city also housed the largest arsenal in the Union, as well as the U.S. Navy Yard and the Baltimore and Ohio railway depot, which moved thousands of troops into and out of the city daily. Washington served as the main supply depot for the Army of the Potomac, which required 10,000 soldiers and civilians to supply it. The city hosted an array of prisons for captured Confederates and disloyal northerners. The Old Capitol Prison, the largest, sat across the street from the Capitol building and held over 2,700 prisoners at its peak.

Along with preservation of the Union, the centerpiece of Lincoln's war effort was, of course, freedom for America's four million slaves. During the war, forty thousand fugitive slaves fled to the nation's capital, hoping to secure their own freedom and hasten emancipation for those they left behind. Dubbed "contrabands" in recognition of their ambiguous legal status (they were originally "confiscated" as "contraband of war"), they set up "freedom villages"—relief camps run by the government, churches, and private charitable organizations—and worked on the city's military projects. Thousands of them eagerly joined the Union army after Lincoln's Emancipation Proclamation allowed them to enlist beginning in 1863. Washington organized two regiments of African American soldiers over the course of the war. Fittingly, the city also helped lead the nation's movement toward emancipation. In April 1862, Lincoln signed the Compensated Emancipation Act, which freed the District of Columbia's three thousand slaves. Thirteen years earlier, as a U.S. congressman from Illinois, Lincoln had introduced an emancipation measure in Congress, a much milder version that received no support. Now his desire to end slavery in the nation's capital became a reality.

Abraham Lincoln envisioned Washington as a key symbol of the American nation, and he worked diligently to turn that idea into a reality.   He not only ensured the security of the capital but turned its proximity to the war to his own advantage. As commander-in-chief, he developed a "hands-on" approach to military strategy, making thirteen trips to meet with his commanders in the field in Virginia and Maryland. On these excursions to the front, Lincoln spent up to a week at a time advising his generals in person, raising morale by reviewing and rallying the troops, visiting with the wounded, and emphasizing his practical and symbolic engagement with the armies as a visible proponent of national resolve. On one occasion, he gained personal insight into the sacrifices the war entailed by witnessing firsthand the burial of the dead on the battlefield. During his presidency, Lincoln spent a total of fifty-eight days away from Washington on these visits to his generals and their troops. Closer at hand, the federal government boasted a mere ten buildings in the city at the outbreak of war. (The number eventually exceeded four hundred.) The headquarters of the War Department sat just a short walk from the White House. The Navy Department, the Union Army Headquarters, the Army of the Potomac Headquarters, and the Headquarters Defenses of Washington all sprang up within walking distance of the White House, providing Lincoln the opportunity to practice his favorite and most effective administrative strategy— "management by walking around." Through his very accessibility in the wartime city, he put his own life at risk to set the right example. By the end of the war, he had helped transform Washington into a truly national capital. Most visibly, Lincoln insisted that work continue without interruption on the unfinished dome of the Capitol building, as the symbol of democracy—"government by the people."

Mary Lincoln believed that she, too, bore a vital civic responsibility. She considered the White House an important symbol of national power and pride, more crucial than ever during a civil war. She was determined to restore the building, which had fallen into considerable disrepair, to its former grandeur, adopting President Jefferson's stately but elegant adornments and entertainments as her model. (Indeed, a statue of Jefferson stood on the front lawn to welcome visitors onto the White House grounds.) Yet a higher goal was to set a tone and in fact a standard of grace and refinement that the entire nation might envy and emulate as befitting the chief executive of a nation that, as her husband put it, was "worth fighting for." Mary Lincoln was determined to use every resource at her disposal to help elevate the presidency that her husband now occupied and to truly earn the novel label "First Lady of the Land." (Although used informally on occasion as early as her distant relative Dolley Madison's tenure in the White House, the label "First Lady" first appeared in print in 1863, with reference to Mary Lincoln.) Mary's education in Lexington and years of experience at Eighth and Jackson in Springfield had prepared her to preside as hostess at the most elegant address in America.

The White House

From their first day in the White House, the Lincolns lived in a home that was surrounded by an armed guard of soldiers and, once the war began, was literally under siege. After escorting the Lincolns from the inaugural ceremony to their new residence, General-in-Chief Winfield Scott ordered the building surrounded by soldiers and then sighed in relief that "Thank God, we now have a government." After the firing on Fort Sumter in April, General Scott even recommended that Mary and her two youngest sons, Willie and Tad, return to Springfield for fear of a Confederate attack on the city. Sitting in his White House office, which faced southward, the new president looked out the window and saw a Confederate flag waving just across the Potomac River in Alexandria, Virginia. He stood at the window day after day waiting for troops to arrive from the North to reinforce the nearly defenseless city and asked in desperation, "Why don't they come? Why don't they come?" In May, the Lincolns' personal friend, the youthful Colonel Elmer Ellsworth, led the 11th New York Volunteer Infantry across the river to retake Alexandria. Ellsworth pulled down the infamous Confederate flag but was shot and killed in the effort. He lay in state in the White House, and Lincoln wrote the first of the moving condolence letters that he would pen to the families of fallen Union soldiers through the next four years of war.

The front of the White House during the Lincoln administration, with the statue of Thomas Jefferson facing north toward Pennsylvania Avenue and Lafayette Square. Library of Congress.

The White House was known formally as the "Executive Mansion," the name that graced Abraham Lincoln's letterhead throughout the course of his presidency (as it did until President Theodore Roosevelt replaced it with "White House" in 1901). Before coming to Washington, Lincoln had never before written the phrase "White House" in any of his letters or speeches that have survived, but within two months of moving in he wrote a memo referring to "what is called the White House." After that, he began to use the label more freely and frequently, emphasizing the simplicity, rather than splendor, of the home that, as he put it, he temporarily occupied. As he told the 166th Ohio Regiment, "I happen temporarily to occupy this big

White House. I am a living witness that any one of your children may look to come here as my father's child has."

The Lincolns settled into the White House quite quickly. The Executive Mansion mimicked their Victorian home in Springfield through its mingling of both public and private areas and functions, albeit on a much grander scale. The first floor was entirely public in character and, in fact, with only a single doorkeeper to monitor and announce visitors, the general public had virtually the run of all the "state chambers," ranging from the State Dining Room on the west end through the Green Room, Blue Room, and Red Room and on to the cavernous East Room, which hosted public receptions and performances. In August 1861, Prince Napoleon of France visited the White House and observed in amazement that "one goes right in as if entering a café." Abraham Lincoln worked upstairs on the second floor in a massive 25 × 40 foot room (now known as the Lincoln Bedroom). This space doubled as his office and the cabinet's meeting room. Lincoln's cabinet included only seven members, so the heavy walnut table at the center of his office could easily accommodate them all at their weekly Tuesday afternoon meetings. A sofa and two chairs lined one of the walls, with military maps hanging above. Lincoln worked at an old mahogany desk in one corner, above which pigeonholes facilitated his idiosyncratic filing system. (One of the pigeonholes contained eighty threatening letters that his secretaries considered serious enough to pass along.) Lincoln personally selected a portrait of Andrew Jackson to hang overhead. A longtime critic of Jackson's imperious exercise of executive authority, as president Lincoln nevertheless admired his predecessor's impassioned and persuasive devotion to the Union.

Previous first families had allowed the White House to deteriorate over time, rarely spending all or even most of the funds that Congress provided for upkeep and improvements. Still, the home boasted several genteel refinements. Gas had just been added to the building to supplement the traditional candlelight. Abraham Lincoln's office had two gas jets with glass globes high on the walls. A furnace in the basement relieved the household from tending the inefficient and unsafe fireplaces, with the attendant soot, that graced all of its rooms. Running water had just been added to the family quarters. Each bedroom had a sink with a faucet, and the family had two toilets in their second-floor family quarters. The water came directly from the Potomac River. A new layer of white paint on the exterior made the White House whiter than ever. Abraham Lincoln's predecessor, James Buchanan, had made another positive addition to the home, a greenhouse on the west end—the new White House Conservatory, which became Mary Lincoln's favorite locale. She delighted in brightening the home with floral arrangements, especially during social functions, presenting bouquets to visitors, and sending flowers to the hospitals to cheer the wounded soldiers. "The conservatory attached to this house is so delightful," she confided in a friend. "We have so many choice bouquets."

Once in the White House, Mary Lincoln quickly assembled a new White House staff that included Mary Ann Cuthbert, who served as both a seamstress and a "dressing maid" and eventually rose to the position of head housekeeper. Two African American women, Rosetta Wells and Hannah Brooks, performed "plain sewing" for the First Lady. Rebecca Pomroy served as the family's nurse. Mary's most important personal assistant and later trusted confidante was Elizabeth Keckly (or Keckley, as it is often spelled), who began as one of her dressmakers but quickly attained the status of "regular modiste." Keckly was a slave for the first thirty-five years of her life. A talented seamstress, she was able to purchase her own freedom and that of her son, who was later killed fighting in the Union army. Relocating to Washington, she built an exclusive clientele that included the future president of the Confederacy, Jefferson Davis, and his wife, Varina. Mary Lincoln hired her on the strength of her reputation, considered her "a very remarkable woman," and grew to depend on her even more for her advice and companionship than for her considerable skills as a dressmaker.

As for Abraham Lincoln, his valet, William H. Johnson, had accompanied the family to Washington, tending to the president-elect during the twelve-day railway journey. Lincoln planned to employ Johnson as a servant and messenger in the White House, but the African American staff objected to him as too dark-skinned. "These servants were so clannish that they even boycotted new employees," according to one reminiscence, "for they were jealous and fearful of their jobs when a new President took office." Lincoln reluctantly yielded and put Johnson to work as a fireman tending the White House furnace. Three days after moving into the White House, he began recommending Johnson for more appropriate positions, telling Secretary of the Navy Gideon Welles that "The difference of color between him & the other servants is the cause of our seperation." In November 1861, he was still trying and wrote to Secretary of the Treasury Salmon Chase that "If you find him a place [I] shall really be obliged." Johnson secured a job as a messenger in the Treasury Department but continued to work for Lincoln as a valet and barber in the mornings. When Lincoln went to Gettysburg in November 1863, he took Johnson with him. After returning, both men contracted smallpox. Lincoln survived but Johnson died of the disease. Lincoln had him buried in Washington's Congressional Cemetery. In Johnson's place, he appointed William Slade, an African American who kept a boardinghouse in Washington and was serving as a messenger in the Treasury Department. Slade became Lincoln's valet and "confidential messenger" and had access to his own carriage to convey private presidential messages around the city by hand. According to his daughter, "He was really a confidential and constant companion and was treated by Lincoln with the greatest intimacy." In July 1866, when Congress established the position of White House steward, Lincoln's successor, Andrew Johnson, appointed Slade to the post, which put him in charge of the entire White House staff.

In Illinois, Mary had always depended heavily on female companionship to relieve her inveterate loneliness and stave off her fear of impending abandonment. True to form, she invited a dozen of her relatives to visit Washington during her first month as First Lady. Back in Springfield, her best friend Mercy Levering Conkling observed with some exaggeration that "Half the town seems to have gone to Washington." She gained the greatest comfort from her oldest sister, Elizabeth Edwards, and her cousin, Elizabeth Todd Grimsley, or "Cousin Lizzie," who spent the most time with her in Washington over the course of the war. Lizzie originally planned to spend a month or so in Washington but ended up keeping Mary company for half a year. Mary also cultivated some of the most powerful men in her husband's administration, offering the kinds of character assessments of potential appointees at which she believed she excelled. To Lincoln's campaign manager, David Davis, she counseled against a cabinet appointment for Chicago newspaperman Norman Judd. "*Judd* would cause trouble & dissatisfaction," she insisted, especially as she put it "in *these times*, when honesty in high places is so important." She was particularly anxious to have the right kind of men overseeing the White House grounds and budget. She reported to Ward Hill Lamon that the applicants for commissioner of public buildings "are very unsuitable, deficient in intelligence, manners, and it may be, morals. May I ask the favor of you, to speak to Mr L. on the subject." She usually got her way but made enemies in the process.

Although Abraham Lincoln now worked at home for the first time during the couple's marriage, his wife and family saw less of him than ever. "The number of times that Mrs. Lincoln herself entered his business-room at the White House," according to one of his secretaries, "could probably be counted on the fingers of one hand." Although his office was just a few steps away from the family quarters, his new responsibilities were vast, and the Lincolns continued to observe the rigid Victorian separation of home and work. The president began with two private secretaries, John Nicolay and John Hay, both of whom came with him from Illinois. They had offices adjacent to his on the second floor of the building and actually lived there, sharing a bedroom to assist Lincoln as necessary twenty-four hours a day. A bell cord hung in Lincoln's office to summon them whenever needed. One of their primary responsibilities was screening the literally thousands of office seekers—and later pardon seekers—who continually haunted the White House's hallways and stairways, hoping to see the president. His doorkeeper (and bodyguard) observed that "Lincoln seldom if ever declined to receive any man or woman who came to the White House to see him." The ever mischievous and enterprising Tad set up a toll gate and solicited donations, five cents apiece, from the waiting supplicants, to support improvements in medical care in the army.

The initial crush of supplicants required Lincoln to keep a twelve-hour day, from breakfast until late evening. Eventually, he could limit his daily reception hours to five (10:00 A.M.–3:00 P.M.) and finally a mere three (10:00 A.M.–1:00 P.M.). Lincoln spent most mornings and evenings in his office attending to the crush of wartime business. "The President's capacity for work was wonderful," remembered one of his secretaries. "Each hour he was busy." The president made two concessions to preserve his family's privacy and provide a few more moments of time alone with them. First, he erected a partition in the reception room that allowed him to slip from his office into the family quarters without being seen, which was the only change that he ordered to the White House during his presidency. Second, he insisted that Nicolay and Hay take all of their meals a few blocks away at the Willard Hotel to avoid any unnecessary intrusions into the family's meals, which they took in the State Dining Room. One unfortunate oversight in the White House's accommodations was the lack of a direct telegraph connection. Lincoln, who made innovative use of telegraphic communications to centralize control over his burgeoning and far-flung army, had to walk next door to the War Department to read messages from the field. There, he spent days on end poring over reports from the field. He soon mastered the art of coordinating a modern army via the recently invented telegraph. During major engagements, he spent many a night huddled in the telegraph office reading and writing dispatches and anxiously waiting for news to arrive. On top of all of her other apprehensions, Mary Lincoln had to worry constantly about her husband's safety as he trudged back and forth to the telegraph office at least twice a day throughout the war.

Just like the Lincoln home at Eighth and Jackson in Springfield, the White House quickly became a playground for Willie and Tad. Abraham and Mary Lincoln cherished their boys beyond measure and gave them the run of the White House, often to the consternation of the president's secretaries and other officials. The Lincolns hired a tutor for the boys and turned the family's second-floor sitting room, the Oval Room, into a makeshift schoolroom during the afternoons. They discovered that the head of the Patent Office, Judge Horatio Taft, had two sons about the same age as Willie and Tad. They invited the Taft boys—Horatio Jr., called Bud, and Halsey, called Holly—to play. The four immediately became fast friends and nearly constant companions. Bud and Holly's older sister, Julia Taft, was sixteen and often accompanied her brothers to the White House, to the delight of Abraham Lincoln, who loved to tease her, and even more so Mary, who had always wanted a daughter. The family included the three Taft children in their school lessons, as well as in many of their more private moments together. Julia, understandably, was willing to withdraw from Madame Smith's French school to join her brothers in the White House, where she undoubtedly learned a lot from Mary Lincoln. Julia later reminisced that beyond their lessons in the Oval Room, the Lincolns resolved simply to "let the children have a good time" in the White House. "Often I have heard Mrs. Lincoln say this with a smile," she remembered, "as her two sons and my two brothers rushed tumultuously through the room, talking loudly of some plan for their amusement." William Slade's daughter Katherine, or "Nibbie," reminisced that she and the other two Slade children often visited the White House, where "they would spend the entire day playing with Tad in the basement, in the White House grounds, or in any other part of the house that the little son of the President wanted to use." Lincoln often returned these visits to the Slades' home and left Tad behind "to spend the entire day with the children and their playmates on Massachusetts Avenue." According to Katherine Slade, "Tad played with all the children and he was a real boy in the midst of real boys and girls, white and colored."

The boys had the run of the White House, its grounds, and in fact beyond. On the White House roof, which Julia Taft labeled "the favorite playground of the boys," they mustered with decommissioned rifles to watch for any enemy advance. "Let 'em come," Tad boasted. "Willie and I are ready for 'em." Deep in the basement of the Capitol building, much to their horror, they discovered rats. Surrounded by an armed guard and thousands of bivouacked soldiers, most of their games quite predictably assumed a military theme. Julia Taft remembered the boys getting hold of six loaded muskets stored in the Taft home and firing one out the bathroom window. The bullet hit the next-door neighbors' house, just missing their maid.

Tad was the youngest and most mischievous of the brothers. His most well known exploits were designed to draw his distracted father into the boys' games. (Julia Taft recalled his disappointment whenever he reported that "Pa don't have time to play with us now.") When Tad prepared to execute the toy soldier Jack for falling asleep on guard duty, for example, Abraham Lincoln intervened to grant him a pardon. This humorous interlude must have brightened the day for the president who had to make hundreds of real life-and-death decisions of that character. Tad's most embarrassing prank was waving a Confederate flag, in fact the same one that Elmer Ellsworth had seized in Alexandria at the cost of his life, on the White House grounds. During a troop review, Tad stood behind his father waving the stars and bars until Lincoln noticed and put an end to the display. Usually, however, the Lincolns tolerated and sometimes abetted Tad's misadventures, especially after Willie died early in 1862. When Tad wanted goats, the Lincolns bought him a pair, Nanny and Nanko, who had the run of the South Lawn. Tad chased them through the gardener's flowerbeds and drove them, pulling an overturned chair, through the East Room. The Lincolns and Mary Ann Cuthbert, their housekeeper, tolerated the animals until Mary and Tad took an extended trip and left Nanny in their care. "Tell dear Tad, poor 'Nanny Goat,' is lost," Abraham wrote Mary, "and Mrs. Cuthbert & I are in distress about it. The day you left Nanny was found resting herself, and chewing her little cud, on the middle of Tad's bed. But now she's gone! The gardener kept complaining that she destroyed the flowers, till it was concluded to bring her down to the White House. This was done, and the second day she had disappeared, and has not been heard of since. This is the last we know of poor 'Nanny.'" The president's message, which he entitled "Letter about 'Nanny goat,'" raises the suspicion that Nanny did not disappear entirely of her own volition. The following year, however, Abraham telegraphed Mary to "Tell Tad the goats and father are very well—especially the goats."

Abraham and Mary Lincoln's seemingly endless toleration for Tad's whimsies clearly tried and even angered the White House staff, but to little avail. After his only recorded argument with his father, Robert Lincoln described a confrontation in which he complained about his parents' overindulgence toward his youngest brother. In his diary, John Hay suggested that Robert lost the argument and felt hurt by the episode. In more tender moments, however, the president enjoyed quiet moments together with his children. Julia Taft remembered Lincoln spending time in the Oval Room in a familiar role, as storyteller, with all of the boys. "Tad perched precariously on the back of the big chair, Willie on one knee, Bud on the other, both leaning against him," she recalled. "Holly usually found a place on the arm of the chair, and often I would find myself swept into the group by the long arm which seemed to reach almost across the room."

The greatest drawback to life in the White House, which had tragic consequences, was sanitation. Of the city's 230 streets, only one was paved, Pennsylvania Avenue, known simply as "the Avenue," which ran from the Capitol northwestward to the White House. In between these two centers of power, the Avenue boasted the city's central marketplace and most fashionable shops, as well as the notorious red-light district popularly known as Murder Bay. Like Centre Market, the White House backed up on the Washington Canal, which had once been a free-flowing creek. Now the canal did double duty as the city's sewage system, channeling the runoff of human and animal waste into the Potomac River. Flowing along what is now Constitution Avenue just south of the White House (an old gatehouse still stands there as part of the White House grounds), the canal emptied into the Potomac at the "watergate" (which lent its name to the now infamous Watergate complex that currently occupies the site). The South Lawn, labeled the White Yard in honor of its conspicuous white picket fence, was essentially Willie and Tad's backyard and sloped downward toward this pestilent canal. Just south of the canal, the mall around the half-finished Washington Monument was a fenced-in pasture containing a cattle grazing area and slaughterhouses to feed the thousands of soldiers who were defending the city. Abraham Lincoln's office looked southward over this scene, with its attendant smells, flies, and mosquitoes. Mary Lincoln complained to a friend that "*dust*, I presume we will never be freed from, until *mud*, takes its place." The refined John Hay simply dubbed the Executive Mansion the "White pest-house."

The Potomac had always been tidal, brackish, and malarial. Now the war aggravated its dangers. In peacetime, an aqueduct carried fresh water from Maryland across the Potomac and into the city. As a military measure, the army commandeered the aqueduct and converted it into a bridge to carry troops and wagons into occupied Virginia, eliminating the fresh water supply for the now tripled population of the city. Compounding this folly, the Union army on the Virginia side dispensed with latrines and instead dug ditches to facilitate the runoff of sewage into the river. This was the water that flowed from the faucets in all of the Lincolns' bedrooms. During his two years in the White House, Willie suffered measles, scarlet fever, and typhoid fever, from which he died. Tad survived measles, typhoid fever, and malaria, for which he took quinine daily. Washington's police repeatedly discovered smallpox victims on Pennsylvania Avenue not far from the White House. "Persons are daily seen on the avenues, in the cars, not only with traces of the disease, but with the disease itself," the *National Republican* reported in November 1863, four days before Lincoln left for Gettysburg. "We heard the other day of one who caught the disease by being jostled against a small-pox patient on Pennsylvania avenue." One U.S. senator died from smallpox. Life in Washington, D.C., was so notoriously dangerous that the British Foreign Office considered its embassy a hardship posting.

Controversy

Mary Lincoln's first forays into the Washington social scene could not have gone better. The inaugural festivities—an afternoon reception at the White House followed by an inaugural ball—were both well-attended, and Mary was beautifully dressed, thanks to the dressmaking entourage that she had so painstakingly assembled. At the ball, all eyes were on Mary as she savored her first dance on the arm of her ironic partner for the evening—Senator Stephen A. Douglas. Always careful to defer to the lady of the house, Lincoln slipped out at 1:00 A.M. and left the Todd women to celebrate until dawn. Four days later, the Lincolns hosted the first social event of their own devising, an evening reception, or "levee," at the White House. Ironically, in light of future events, Washingtonians were initially more apprehensive about Mary Lincoln's *western* heritage than her *southern* roots. Harriet Lane, Buchanan's niece, for example, feared that she would prove "awfully *western*, loud & unrefined." The levee, however, went well and earned widespread praise as a "monstrous success" and the "most successful party" ever held at the White House.

Mary Lincoln as White House hostess; carte de visite from photograph taken by Mathew Brady in 1861. Library of Congress.

One of the First Lady's formal duties was hosting a demanding social schedule, including a round of presidential levees at which attendance was virtually unrestricted. "The President's Receptions are every other Tuesday evening, and the attendance of all his constituents is expected, without cards of invitation," the *Daily National Republican* announced, "limited, of course, to the capacity of the White House, which, however, holds an immense number." The Tuesday evening receptions ran from 8:30 to 11:00. Mary Lincoln also held her own Saturday Matinee between 1:00 and 3:00, again with attendance unrestricted. The Matinee occurred weekly, and the president was expected to attend as well, "when his public duties permit." Mary's private entertainments were equally popular. During her first month in Washington, she could boast that "This is certainly a very charming spot & I have formed many delightful acquaintances. Every evening our *blue room*, is filled with the elite of the land, last eve, we had about 40 to call in, to see us *ladies*." She wrote a friend cheerfully that "I am beginning to feel so perfectly at home, and enjoy every thing so much."

With the outbreak of civil war, Washington society's and indeed the nation's mood changed overnight. Both sides, North and South, Unionists and Confederates, found reason to distrust Mary Lincoln. Southerners saw a traitor to her section who left for the North, married a Republican "abolitionist," and now helped preside over a war of aggression against the South. Northerners suspected her for a secret southern sympathizer with deep roots in the slave South and a family full of not only Rebel supporters but Confederate soldiers as well. In truth, the younger of Mary's full brothers, George, served in the Confederate army, as did all three of her half brothers. Another three of her half sisters were married to Confederate officers, including Emilie, whose husband, Benjamin Hardin Helm, was a Confederate general. Betsey Todd, Mary's stepmother, was a distant relative of John C. Breckinridge, the Southern Democratic nominee for president in 1860 and Confederate major general of the 1st Kentucky Brigade. (Before the firing on Fort Sumter, Mary had entertained him in the White House.) In short, her southern, slave-owning heritage and the bitter division of the Todd family now caught Mary Lincoln in the middle between the two warring sections. Julia Taft put it bluntly: "Mrs. Lincoln was wickedly maligned by people saying that she was in sympathy with the South."

Mary's answer was simple and straightforward. As she remarked to Elizabeth Keckly, "Why should I sympathize with the rebels? Are they not against me? They would hang my husband to-morrow if it was in their power." Later, she told Emilie Helm in a panic that "I seem to be the scape-goat for both North and South." Elizabeth Grimsley noticed that old Washingtonians began to shun the First Lady. Soon, she wrote, "we ceased to meet at our informal receptions the Maryland and Virginia families who had always held sway, and dominated Washington society." Socialite Elizabeth Blair Lee, daughter of Maryland Republican Francis Preston Blair, tried to organize support for the Lincolns. "The women kind are giving Mrs. Lincoln the cold shoulder in the City," she complained, "and consequently we Republicans ought to Rally." The northern press quickly turned on Mary Lincoln, exaggerated her influence on administration policy, and dubbed her "Madame President."

Compounding Mary's troubles, she faced hostility in her own White House. Simply put, Abraham Lincoln's secretaries resented her potential influence with the president. State Department protocol demanded a fixed regimen of formal state dinners, dominated by government officials and foreign dignitaries, which supported a familiar rhythm of sedate White House events throughout the Washington social season. As Abraham Lincoln's private secretary, John Nicolay was charged with overseeing these and all other White House social functions. Mary Lincoln, however, decided to replace the traditional state dinners with a series of three public receptions that she would orchestrate, on the grounds that receptions would be larger, less expensive, and more inclusive. She talked her husband into supporting the plan, which, in the process, undermined Nicolay's authority over the White House social calendar and, by implication, his overall standing with the president. Now expert at shielding Abraham Lincoln from supplicants of all varieties, Nicolay and Hay resolved to protect the president from undue influence from his wife, as well. These two young and overeager secretaries saw themselves, quite patronizingly, as the stewards of the president's time, energies, and indeed best interests, even to the point of denying the First Lady access to her own husband, as they deemed appropriate. They labeled her "the hellcat" and, as the rivalry between the secretaries and the First Lady escalated, John Hay observed that "The Hell-cat is getting more Hell-cattical day by day." In her own turn, Mary grew to resent Nicolay and Hay's exaggerated influence on the president. At last, relief appeared in the person of William O. Stoddard, a clerk in the Interior Department whom Lincoln appointed as his third private secretary. Mary got along famously with Stoddard, whom she called "Stod," and entrusted him with the considerable responsibility of opening her mail. After two-and-a-half years, however, in early 1864, Stoddard took ill and had to leave the White House. During her last year as first lady, Mary made do with her penchant for cultivating cabinet members and influential senators, including Edwin Stanton and Charles Sumner, as White House allies. Toward the end of the war, Nicolay was referring to Mary as "Her Majesty" or even "the enemy."

Even before traveling to Washington for the Inauguration, Mary Lincoln journeyed to New York City to shop. Traveling to the major centers of culture and fashion—Philadelphia, New York City, and Boston—ensured that she would uphold her self-imposed standards of quality and style as a worthy First Lady for the divided nation. Shopping trips gave her the opportunity to escape both the literal and figurative heat of Washington, exercise her symbolic and indeed real authority as the nation's new fashion leader, and attempt to reinstate the White House as a symbol of national pride and, by extension, power. As she explained to her dressmaker, Elizabeth Keckly, "I must dress in costly materials. The people scrutinize every article that I wear with critical curiosity." This was also an arena in which no man, no matter how vain or refined, could compete with her. She shopped not only for herself but for the White House, which she was determined to resurrect to its former glory as a fitting presidential mansion. During her first shopping trip for household furnishings, she brought William Wood, the acting commissioner of public buildings, and her cousin Elizabeth Grimsley with her to New York City. Every president received a $20,000 congressional appropriation for the White House furnishings, for his entire four-year term. Previous first families spent the funds overcautiously, so the White House languished in threadbare condition. Mary Lincoln now went over-board in refurbishing a mansion that she considered something of a national disgrace. Her most expensive purchases were a $2,500 carpet for the expansive East Room, a seven-hundred-piece set of cut glass tableware, a large set of gold-trimmed china, and $6,800 in French wallpaper. She later spent almost $6,000 on silverware, china, and chandeliers through a New York importer and $7,500 on carpeting and wallpaper with a Philadelphia merchant, and this was only the beginning. A rosewood grand piano from Philadelphia facilitated performances at White House entertainments, as well as music les-sons for Willie and Tad.

Her northern forays lasted two, three, or four months at a time, and she usually took one or more of her sons with her, as well as female companions, at first Elizabeth Grimsley and later Elizabeth Keckly. Favoring summers to escape from Washington, she often combined shopping with recuperation in mountain resorts in Ver-mont and New York. As she explained to a friend before fleeing the White House during August 1861, "I have passed through so much excitement, that a change is absolutely necessary." Robert Lincoln would sometimes join his mother and brothers when he could get away from Harvard. During these extended excursions, Abraham and Mary kept in close contact, preferably by telegraph, usually to inquire about the health and safety of their sons. A typical note from Mary read "Your telegram received. Did you receive my reply[?]" A typical reply from her husband read simply "All doing well." So regular was their communication that any interruption was sure to produce anxiety. On one trip to New York, for example, Mary wrote the president impatiently that "I have waited in vain to hear from you, yet as you are not *given* to letter writing, will be charitable enough to impute your silence, to the right cause." She followed this buoyant tone with a mild rebuke: "Strangers come up from W—— & tell me you are well." On a later trip, she telegraphed Lincoln, "Do let me know how Taddie and yourself are," but then promptly telegraphed the White House doorkeeper, "Let me know immediately exactly how Mr. Lincoln and Taddie are." The president was clearly less com-municative, and it might take a succession of messages to provoke a reply, as when he wrote, "Your three despatches received. I am very well; and am glad to know that you & 'Tad' are so." Still, he left no doubt about how much he cherished his family when he dashed off a telegram to Philadelphia that read simply, "Think you better put 'Tad's' pistol away. I had an ugly dream about him."

Increasingly, however, Mary Lincoln wrote to ask her husband to send money. On a trip to New York City in 1864, for example, she telegraphed Abraham, "We reached here in safety. Hope you are well. Please send me by mail to-day a check for $50." As her bills mounted and she overspent the congressional appropriation, Mary Lincoln began to withhold the most damaging information from her husband, the true extent of her outstanding debts to the merchants who were refurbishing the White House. She now entered into informal arrangements, indeed intrigues, with a series of male government officials to procure more funding while hiding her existing indebtedness. The first was the acting public buildings commissioner, William Wood, whose overly familiar relationship with the First Lady raised public suspicions of impropriety that were unfounded but damaging nonetheless. Next, Mary turned to the White House's gardener, John Watt, who was able to hide, at least temporarily, the mounting debts by shifting them to other White House accounts. Finally, she convinced the new commissioner of public buildings, Benjamin Brown French, both to continue these accounting practices and to intercede with the president on her behalf. When he did so, according to French, Abraham Lincoln confronted Mary and railed that "it would stink in the land to have it said that an appropriation of $20,000 for furnishing the house had been overrun by the President when the poor, freezing soldiers could not have blankets, & he swore that he would never approve the bills for *flub dubs for that damned old house*." True to his nickname, Honest Abe, the president felt honor-bound to make good the debt and "pay it out of his own pocket." Eventually, Congress made two additional appropriations to cover the overdrafts. Meanwhile, Lincoln and his secretaries practiced extreme frugality in appointing their offices. A mahogany sofa, six chairs, and four mounted wall maps cost them a total of $44.50.

After losing his struggle with Mary Lincoln to control the White House social schedule, John Nicolay wrote to his fiancée that "'La Reine' has determined to abrogate dinners and institute parties in their stead. How it will work remains to be seen." Mary scheduled the first of the three receptions for February 5, 1862. The large, public gathering was meant to show off the lavish renovations to which she had devoted the White House budget—and more. "Half the city is jubilant at being invited," John Hay quipped with seeming satisfaction, "while the other half is furious at being left out in the cold." When Senator Benjamin Wade, chairman of the Joint Committee on the Conduct of the War, received his invitation, he asked "Are the President and Mrs. Lincoln aware that there is a civil war?" He then declined the invitation. In the end, the Lincolns expanded the guest list to make the affair even more inclusive and paid for it out of the president's private funds. Undeterred, Mary prepared a flowing white silk dress with bare shoulders and a plunging back in the style of the French Empress Eugenie, the current exemplar of European fashion. Critics joined Senator Wade in faulting her for holding a gala in the midst of a bloody and costly civil war and, when her son Willie contracted typhoid fever, the same disease that had claimed Prince Albert two months earlier, she took it as divine retribution for her heedless pride and extravagance.

Both Willie and Tad contracted typhoid fever that winter, probably through the new plumbing that piped Potomac River water into their bedrooms. Tad recovered, but Willie had suffered measles and scarlet fever the previous winter, which undoubtedly weakened his immune system and left his body more susceptible to the ravages of the typhoid. Both parents suffered grievously after Willie's death, but Abraham Lincoln had a war to manage and could not indulge the kind of debilitating depression he had experienced twice before in New Salem and Springfield, his famous "crazy spells." Mary, however, succumbed to predictable "paroxysms of grief" and spent the next three weeks virtually incapacitated in bed. According to Elizabeth Keckly, who emerged as Mary's closest companion during this period of prolonged mourning, President Lincoln—himself devastated by Willie's death—led her to a window, pointed toward the city's lunatic asylum, and warned her, "Try and control your grief or it will drive you mad and we may have to send you there." Mary well knew the Christian consolation literature that enjoined survivors to place their faith in God and look forward to a heavenly reunion with the departed, condemning excessive mourning as evidence of a doubter's lack of faith. Such a refusal to submit to God's will was itself a defiant act of pride. Still, Mary Lincoln practiced mourning with a vengeance. Banishing all mementoes of Willie, she shipped his belongings back to Springfield and even excluded his playmates Bud and Holly Taft from the White House forever. Emulating Queen Victoria, she ordered lavish mourning regalia, black crepe dresses, bonnets, and veils, and even black jewelry, insisting on the "blackest" and dullest crepe available from the suppliers of mourning goods that had sprung up in the big cities as the war dragged on. Although mourning manuals called for six months of mourning after the death of a child, Mary insisted on observing first-degree mourning for an entire year, after which she entered half-mourning, wearing gray and then lavender with a "touch of white at the wrist" for another six months. Her sister, Elizabeth Edwards, who visited the White House to console her, concluded with sympathetic understatement that "Mary is so constituted as to present a long indulgence of such gloom."

In her efforts to see and talk with Willie again, and perhaps to make amends for the false pride that she believed had contributed to his death, Mary turned to spiritualism for comfort. Washington was rife with spiritualists during the Civil War, representing a legitimate part of the Victorian grieving process but also the kind of mercenary opportunism that sometimes accompanies widespread death. Spiritualists specialized in promising communication with departed family members, usually children, and appealed particularly to women as wives and mothers. The endorsements by and examples of Horace Greeley, editor of the *New York Tribune*, Harriet Beecher Stowe, Secretary of the Navy Gideon Welles, and even her predecessor as First Lady, Mrs. Franklin Pierce, all of whom consulted spiritualists to contact their deceased children, lent both popularity and legitimacy to the practice. After Willie's death, Mary Lincoln patronized the city's mediums routinely and even invited spiritualists into the White House. In all, she held eight recorded séances in the White House and at least one at the Soldiers' Home, some of which her husband himself attended. Abraham Lincoln asked Dr. Joseph Henry, secretary of the Smithsonian Institution, one of the country's leading scientists and a personal friend, to investigate the validity of the séances. Henry investigated and revealed how the most effective of the psychics, known as Lord Colchester, was able to project sounds across a darkened room with a hidden apparatus. After his wife offered him political and military advice on the basis of her contact with the other side, Lincoln used his presidential power to curb the visits and warn off the spiritualists.

Willie Lincoln, third son of Abraham and Mary Lincoln, shortly before his death at age eleven; carte de visite from photograph taken by Mathew Brady in 1862. Library of Congress.

After the shock of Willie's death, Mary Lincoln had abandoned her loftiest ambitions for the White House and settled more comfortably into the role of a traditional First Lady. She did an about-face on the subject of entertaining at the White House, satisfied to reinstate the more sedate routine of state dinners and small gatherings that previous administrations had maintained. She kept her extravagance under check and spent more of her annual summer excursions vacationing in Saratoga, New York, or Manchester, Vermont, rather than shopping in New York City. Ominously for the future, she began to scrimp on expenditures, bargain with shopkeepers, and horde household supplies. At one point, she asked the gardener to sell manure from the White House stables as fertilizer. Near the end of her husband's term, she told Elizabeth Keckly that she still owed $27,000 to merchants for her earlier purchases, a sum that exceeded his annual presidential salary. Mary Lincoln probably stopped consulting spiritualists, certainly inviting them into the White House, by mid-1863, a year or so after Willie died. Still, she could never escape the torments that all too often accompany motherhood. When Emilie Todd Helm visited the White House late in 1863, her sister Mary woke her up one night to announce that "He lives, Emilie! He comes to me every night and stands at the foot of my bed with the same sweet, adorable smile he always had." In her unrelenting grief, she added that "little Eddie is sometimes with him."

Mary found solace in her relationship with eldest son Robert, who had always felt closer to his mother than to his father. When Robert left Springfield for Harvard in 1859, Mary confided to her friend Hannah Shearer that "I am feeling quite lonely, as Bob, left for College, in Boston, a few days since, and it almost appears, as if light & mirth, had departed with him." A year later, her sense of loss had only deepened, and she wrote another friend that "Our oldest boy, has been absent, almost a *year*, a *long year*, & at times I feel *wild* to see him." Even before her elevation to First Lady, she made plans to vacation with Robert in the White Mountains, and now she included him in her summer excursions at every opportunity. Robert sojourned at the White House, as well, helping to fill the gap left by the loss of Willie. During the summer of 1862, for example, Mary reported to a prominent Washington hostess that "our boy Robert, is with us, whom you may remember. We consider it a 'pleasant time' for us, when his vacations, roll around, he is very companionable, and I shall dread when he has to return to Cambridge."

After losing two sons, Eddie and Willie, both Abraham and Mary Lincoln dismissed any thought of Robert enlisting to help with the war effort. For his part, Robert felt awkward about remaining in college when so many other young men, both volunteers and draftees, were dying on the battlefield, but he deferred to his parents' wishes. With his impending graduation from Harvard, public indignation at his continued civilian status steadily mounted. Still, Robert dutifully enrolled in Harvard's law school to pursue a career in his father's profession. Early in 1865, however, he at last prevailed upon his parents to allow him to enlist. The president sought the advice of General Ulysses S. Grant, who agreed to add Robert to his staff at the rank of captain. The newly commissioned officer selected a horse—with his father's advice—and reported for duty at Grant's field headquarters in Virginia less than two months before the war ended. Two days later, Lincoln, ever the anxious parent, telegraphed Grant in cipher, "I have not heard of my son reaching you." The next day, the politically astute general patiently replied that "Capt Lincoln reported on the 22nd and was assigned to duty at my Head Quarters." Now there was a Lincoln in uniform.

Mary Lincoln, however, and even her husband, never quite managed to convince the public of their thoroughgoing loyalty to the Union, largely because of their charitable sympathy toward their Todd relatives. The balance sheet of Mary's Todd siblings tilted conspicuously toward the Confederacy. Three of her half brothers died fighting for the South, and even her full brother, George Rogers Clark Todd, served the Confederacy as a surgeon in a South Carolina hospital. The fate of Mary's favorite half sister, Emilie Todd Helm, eventually forced the wrenching choice between family connections and national allegiance. During the fall of 1863, Emilie's husband, Confederate general Benjamin Hardin Helm, died at the Battle of Chickamauga. His death dealt a personal blow to the Lincolns, who both felt tremendous affection for both Emilie and Ben, and created a difficult political situation. Ben Helm's father was the wartime governor of Kentucky, a crucial but divided border state. When he sought safe passage for his daughter-in-law to return to Lexington, the president granted it readily. While crossing through Union lines, however, Emilie defiantly refused to take the requisite oath of allegiance to the United States. Lincoln, who harbored fond memories of his sister-in-law from her days as a visitor in his home in Springfield and called her "Little Sister," responded simply "Bring her to me."

Emilie's extended visit to the White House, where she became a welcome companion and confidante for her half sister, provoked open scorn from government and military officials who were fighting and sacrificing in the struggle against the Confederacy. After her undiplomatic defiance prompted resentment and indeed insults from leading Washingtonians, Emilie retreated to Lexington. The president pleaded with her to stay for Mary's benefit, observing that his wife's nerves had "gone to pieces," but in vain. A year later, however, Helm returned to the White House to ask the president, quite brazenly, for a license to sell cotton from her plantation in the South. Lincoln granted the favor on the condition that she at last take the oath of allegiance, which she steadfastly refused to do. From back in Lexington, she wrote Lincoln a letter blaming him for her family's misfortunes, including the deaths of her husband and brothers. Mary Lincoln could never forgive this personal attack on her husband, and the two never met or corresponded again. After the war, Emilie Helm reminisced fondly about Abraham and Mary Lincoln, befriended her nephew Robert, and burned her wartime diary. Remarkably, she lived as a reminder of reconciliation until 1930. For the moment, however, Mary's circle of family and friends continued to diminish as her critics grew in number and resolve.

Refuge

By 1864, Mary Lincoln strove to restore the White House to its former conviviality and did her best to resume her role as a gracious hostess. The Lincolns started off the year with a Tuesday evening levee that surpassed, by all accounts, any of their previous social events. "Between the hours of 8 and 11 o'clock," the *Daily National Republican* reported, "a steady stream of human beings, of all classes in society, the high and low, young and old, beautiful and ugly, rich and poor, bold misses and modest retiring maidens—to the number of about eight thousand, passed the President and Mrs. Lincoln and paid their respects." The newspaper praised Mary Lincoln as "never more richly and tastefully or more appropriately attired" and noted in passing that she "was assisted by Secretary Stoddard in doing the honors of the occasion," while John Nicolay stood at the president's side.

Significantly, the report declared that "We have not seen the President looking in better health than last night." Indeed, after losing Willie and forfeiting her own composure for well over a year, Mary Lincoln now focused on the health and security of her remaining family members—husband Abraham and sons Tad and Robert. After Willie's death, she concluded—and readily admitted—that "I had become, so wrapped up in the world, so devoted to our own political advancement that I thought of little else besides." The war was taking a terrible toll on Abraham Lincoln, who told Harriet Beecher Stowe during her visit to the White House that "I shall never live to see peace. This job is killing me." One of Mary Lincoln's personal prescriptions for her husband was an afternoon carriage ride. Both of them looked forward to the pleasant rides together. As Mary boasted to a friend with feigned humility, "There are so many lovely drives around W. and we have only *three* carriages, at our command." The poet Walt Whitman, who lived in Washington through most of the war, remembered spotting the couple on some of these outings. "Earlier in the summer I occasionally saw the President and his wife, toward the latter part of the afternoon, out in a barouche, on a pleasure ride through the city," he recounted in *Specimen Days*. "Mrs. Lincoln was dress'd in complete black, with a long crape veil." Mary grew particularly crucial in maintaining her husband's health and spirits. When she was away, for example, Lincoln wrote, "have not rode out much yet but at last got new tires on the carriage wheels, & perhaps, shall ride out soon."

Previous first families had spent part of their summers in a cottage at the Soldiers' Home, which sat on the highest point in the District of Columbia and was therefore the coolest and driest locale within commuting distance of the White House. A twenty-two-room Greek Revival cottage on the grounds was available for the Lincolns to occupy as they chose, but during their first summer in

Abraham Lincoln and his ten-year-old son Tad in a typical private moment after the loss of Willie; photograph taken by Anthony Berger on February 9, 1864. Library of Congress.

Washington the family elected to stay in the White House. In 1862, however, after Willie's death and the growing criticism of Mary's role in her husband's presidency, the Lincolns decided to summer at the Soldiers' Home. Mary continued in mourning but benefited from the more pleasant surroundings that Willie had never inhabited. A half hour's carriage ride from the White House, the cottage became a welcome refuge from the heat, humidity, and germs of the city, as well as the lines of office- and favor-seekers who continued to plague the president. He could make a daily commute on horseback or by carriage, arriving at the White House by 8:00 A.M. and returning in the evening, quite often after dusk. Here he found the kind of quiet solitude that he had always needed to think, reflect, and write. He could also entertain his closest friends and advisers in privacy, read his favorite humorists—Petroleum V. Nasby, Artemus Ward, and Orpheus C. Kerr—and pore over his Bible, in which he increasingly sought wisdom and solace as the war progressed. Secretary of War Edwin Stanton also had a cottage on the grounds, and he became a close friend, trusted adviser, and confirmed admirer. All told, Abraham Lincoln spent thirteen months—one-fourth of his presidency—commuting to and from the Soldiers' Home, including ten weeks in the summer of 1863 and six weeks in the summer of 1864, when Mary left Washington to seek out her own personal refuge farther north.

The president traveled a familiar and well-known route as he commuted daily, attracting the gaze of onlookers and well-wishers, which he believed kept him in closer touch with the people. Most famously, Walt Whitman delighted in studying Lincoln's visage as he passed by. He lived along the route that Lincoln followed and saw the president pass around 8:30 A.M. "Mr. Lincoln on the saddle generally rides a good-sized, easy-going gray horse," Whitman recalled, "is dress'd in plain black, somewhat rusty and dusty, wears a black stiff hat, and looks about as ordinary in attire, &c., as the commonest man." The president was typically pensive, and Whitman related perceptively that "I see very plainly Abraham Lincoln's dark brown face, with the deep-cut lines, the eyes, always to me with a deep latent sadness in the expression."

Lincoln's route took him past Camp Barker, Washington's first government-sponsored "contraband camp" or freedom village. The first fugitive slaves who arrived in Washington were considered criminals, even after the war began, and were lodged in Washington's city jail, nicknamed the "slave pen." As they grew in number, they were transferred to the Old Capitol Prison, across the street from the Capitol. Here, they were housed with captured Confederate soldiers, disloyal northerners, and accused spies, some of them in the same boardinghouse that the Lincolns had occupied in 1847–49. After Lincoln personally intervened to "decriminalize" these fugitive slaves, they were transferred to a row of townhouses next door, known as Carroll's Row, that had been confiscated from a Confederate sympathizer. The increasingly crowded conditions bred an outbreak of smallpox, so in 1863 Washington established the first true "contraband camp," Camp Barker, which soon numbered five thousand fugitives and set the pattern for the many "freedom villages" that followed.

The Lincolns' cook at the Soldiers' Home was "Aunt" Mary Dines, a runaway slave who lived at Camp Barker. Dines was born a slave in Prince George's County, Maryland, but fled to Washington, D.C., before the war. By the light of the moon, according to her reminiscence, she "made her getaway, and traveling for many nights with the aid of friendly slaves, she arrived on the Maryland side of the Eastern Branch near the old Navy Yard Bridge." She hid in the straw of a hay-wagon, which was a "pick-up" wagon that took her to one of the "stations" on Washington's Underground Railroad, an "old stable in an alley on Capitol Hill." She blended into the city's large free African American population and worked for a family south of the Washington Canal on the "Island," the poorest district in the city. With the outbreak of war, Dines moved into Camp Barker where, she reminisced, President Lincoln frequently stopped "to visit and talk" with the former slaves on his way to and from the Soldiers' Home. Dines was a talented soprano who led the former slaves in song as Lincoln listened. "He was no President when he came to camp," she emphasized. "He just stood and sang and prayed just like all the rest of the people." On one occasion, according to Dines, the former slaves sang "Swing Low, Sweet Chariot," "Go Down Moses," "Been in the Storm So Long," and other spirituals and hymns. "President Lincoln actually joined in singing every piece," according to her reminiscence, "and he was so tenderhearted that he filled-up when he went over to bid the real old folks good-by."

Mary Dines remembered as well that "Mrs. Lincoln contributed money and sent gifts to the older people" at Camp Barker. Through her deepening connections with African Americans, particularly former slaves such as Mary Dines and Elizabeth Keckly, Mary Lincoln increasingly developed a genuine interest in helping the freedmen. In Springfield, Mary had referred to African Americans crudely as "Kentucky darkies" and thought of them as nothing more than menials under the management of white people. Through her association with African Americans in Washington, she gradually developed a greater appreciation and indeed respect for them as independent individuals. Both of the Lincolns enjoyed confidential relationships with African Americans, including Mary Keckly and William Slade, but growing up in the slave South ironically granted Mary much more experience than her husband in interacting with African Americans, beginning with her "Aunt" Sally, not only as servants but as people. Although Abraham Lincoln supported the emancipation of slaves in Washington in April 1862 and, of course, issued the Emancipation Proclamation in 1863, his wife infused much greater urgency into the necessity of aiding the former slaves.

When Elizabeth Keckly sought support for the city's freedom villages, Mary lent and donated funds to her directly and was eloquent in asking her husband to help as well. Keckly used her trips northward with the First Lady as opportunities to solicit support for her relief efforts from contributors in New York and Philadelphia. In November 1862, for example, Mary wrote to her husband from New York that "Elizabeth Keckley, who is with me and is working for the Contraband Association, at Wash is authorized by the *White* part of the concern by a written document—to collect any thing for them—*here* that, she can—She has been very unsuccessful." Mary went on to report that "the immense number of Contrabands in W——— are suffering intensely, many without bed covering," adding pointedly, "Many dying of want." Then she asked directly, "Please send check for $200," which he did. "The cause of humanity requires it," she assured him. On another occasion, Keckly asked Mary to lend her $30, and Mary asked Abraham Lincoln for $100.

Jane Grey Swisshelm, an abolitionist and feminist reformer, actually concluded that Mary Lincoln was now "more radically opposed to slavery" than even her husband. For his part, the president grew substantially in his relations with African Americans and gained much more understanding and sympathy for their plight. Through Elizabeth Keckly's influence, he met a wider range of African Americans, including Sojourner Truth, who received an invitation to the White House. Lincoln developed a genuine friendship with his "particular friend" Frederick Douglass, who recalled that "In all my interviews with Mr. Lincoln, I was impressed with his entire freedom from popular prejudice against the colored race." Emphasizing the sincerity and impact of this real friendship, on August 11, 1863, the president met with Frederick Douglass and later on the same day wrote a personal check for $5 made out simply to "A Colored Man with one Leg."

Two military hospitals, Harewood and Campbell, also lined the route to the Soldiers' Home, affording both Lincolns the opportunity to stop, visit, and rally the sick and wounded. Louisa May Alcott called Civil War Washington, fittingly, "a camp of hospitals." Both Lincolns paid visits to the city's hospitals, but of course Mary had more time to devote and increasingly identified with the wounded and their families. From the White House, she sent flowers gathered from the "Buchanan greenhouse" and surplus food from the kitchen. She also raised money, including a $1,000 donation during one of her trips to New York City, to buy fruit to help stave off scurvy. In 1864, she contributed flower arrangements to the large Sanitary Fair that took place for the benefit of the Washington hospitals. They were auctioned off and fetched up to $50 apiece. On her visits to the hospitals, she consoled the men, read to them, copied letters home, and attended musical performances and literary readings. In August 1862, a Washington newspaper noted that "Mrs. Lincoln has been quietly engaged, for some weeks, in a systematic visitation of the hospitals of this city and vicinity." The *Boston Daily Journal* reported that "Secesh sympathizers call her the 'hospital matron,' but grateful hearts chronical her errands of mercy to those brave men, who are cheered by her visits and benefited by her liberal donations." On one occasion, she brought flowers to a convalescing soldier at Campbell Hospital. On her next visit, she wrote a letter to his mother. "My dear Mrs Agen," she wrote, "I am sitting by the side of your soldier boy. He has been quite sick, but is getting well. He tells me to say to you that he is all right. With respect for the mother of a young soldier." She signed the letter "Mrs Abraham Lincoln." When the soldier, James Agen, reached home and read the letter, he told his family that he had no idea that his visitor had been Mary Lincoln. As one of the newspapers put it, "Among the many ladies who visit the hospitals none is more indefatigable than Mrs. Lincoln."

To accommodate the thousands of hospital patients who did not recover, the government established the first national military cemetery at the Soldiers' Home. Surely the dreary sight of this nearby cemetery accepting its pine coffins day by day, a total of eight thousand, moved both the Lincolns to action. After it filled up, Abraham Lincoln suggested, with ironic justice, Robert E. Lee's estate across the Potomac River at Arlington as a more poignant resting place. For the next two years, coffins moved solemnly, by the hundreds, across the Long Bridge and over the Potomac to what became Arlington National Cemetery. The government also established two new freedom villages on the Lee estate, next to the new Arlington National Cemetery, one of which endured until 1890.

The Soldiers' Home relieved the Lincolns from a variety of troubles in the White House but exposed them to still other physical dangers. Kidnapping and assassination plots increasingly focused opportunistically on the Soldiers' Home. After the war, Thomas Nelson Conrad of the Confederate Signal Corps revealed his involvement in a conspiracy to kidnap Lincoln during his daily commute. John Wilkes Booth's initial plan was to kidnap Lincoln while he was commuting to and from the Soldiers' Home. He later proposed abducting the president while he was visiting Campbell Hospital. In September 1862, Lincoln put General George McClellan in command of Washington's defenses. McClellan sensibly installed a military guard at the Soldiers' Home. Lincoln initially made his daily ride unescorted and without any protection. "A stranger to fear," Marshal Ward Hill Lamon recalled, "he often eluded our vigilance; and before his absence could be noted he would be well on his way to his summer residence, alone, and many times at night." On one occasion, Lamon arrived at the White House only to learn that Lincoln had ridden off on his favorite horse, "Old Abe." Fearing an assassination attempt, Lamon borrowed the fastest horse on the grounds and rode after him. Fortunately, the president's horse "wouldn't go faster than a dogtrot if you beat him to death," so Lamon caught up with both Old Abes halfway to the Soldiers' Home. "Lincoln, far from suspecting that the Marshal was on his trail," according to reminiscence, "invited him to come along and have some fun."

The recently restored Lincoln family summer cottage at the Soldiers' Home in Washington, D.C.; photograph taken by Carol M. Highsmith on January 27, 2009. Library of Congress.

On another occasion, sentries at the Soldiers' Home heard a gunshot and were startled to see the president, on horseback, speed onto the grounds without his trademark stovepipe hat. When they investigated, they found the hat shot through with a conspicuous bullet hole. Lincoln blamed the episode on a careless hunter—"some foolish gunner"—and shrugged off any concerns for his safety. The next day, he told Lamon about the episode, which he tried to laugh off while admitting that "just now I don't know what to think: I am staggered." Lamon concluded that "he was always prepared for the inevitable, and singularly indifferent as to his personal safety."

At both Mary Lincoln's and Ward Hill Lamon's insistence, General James Wadsworth, military governor of the District of Columbia, assigned a mounted regiment, the 11th New York Cavalry, as Lincoln's escort. "He always has a company of twenty-five or thirty cavalry, with sabres drawn and held upright over their shoulders," Walt Whitman observed. "They say this guard was against his personal wish, but he let his counselors have their way." Lincoln considered the escort an unnecessary barrier to his contact with the public. He complained to his general in chief, Henry Halleck, that "he and Mrs. Lincoln 'couldn't hear themselves talk,' for the clatter of their sabers and spurs." Drawing on humor to defuse concerns over his safety, he claimed that "he was more afraid of being shot by the accidental discharge of one of their carbines or revolvers, than of any attempt upon his life."

Ominously, the dangers were all too real. In July 1863, Mary Lincoln was riding in a carriage near Mount Pleasant Hospital when the coachman's seat came loose and threw him onto the ground. When the horses ran off with the carriage, the First Lady jumped out and hit her head as she fell onto the roadway. The wound festered and the infection spread. Her already bothersome headaches increased in frequency, and Robert Lincoln believed that his mother never entirely recovered. This suspicious accident may well have targeted the president, but Abraham Lincoln typically minimized the episode. His only official response was a memo directing that "The place on the road near Mt. Pleasant Hospital ought to be repaired."

The White House itself was hardly much safer. Throughout the war, uniformed soldiers secured the entrances. Toward the end of the war, the Washington police posted four plainclothes policemen in the White House who posed as doorkeepers and valets but were in fact a presidential bodyguard. Ward Hill Lamon, known as "Hill" because of his burly physique, acted in that capacity as well and was seen sleeping on the floor in front of the president's bedroom with a loaded pistol in each hand. The White House grounds were literally an army camp, hosting among other units Company K of the 150th Pennsylvania Infantry on the South Lawn. But even this shield was all too porous. According to reminiscence, Lamon was making his nightly rounds of the White House grounds when he noticed movement in the shrubbery. He "reached the spot by three leaps, faced a dark figure and, without ado, dealt him a blow square between the eyes." The single blow purportedly killed the intruder, who was carrying two pistols and two knives and was found to hail from a distinguished southern family. In February 1864, Abraham Lincoln discovered a fire in the White House stable. He raised the alarm, but the recently formed city fire department could not put out the flames. The stable and all six horses were lost, including two belonging to the president, two of John Nicolay's, and two that were kept for Tad. The Lincolns were particularly heartbroken because one of the horses that Tad rode had been their son Willie's favorite. Detectives concluded that the fire had been set intentionally, but the perpetrator and motive were never established. The White House remained so insecure that the commissioner of public buildings reported rampant theft and vandalism and requested appointment of a watchman in December 1864.

When the war ended on April 9, 1865, the Lincoln family, quite understandably, rejoiced and let down their guard completely. Five days later, hours before he was assassinated, Abraham Lincoln accompanied Mary on one of their familiar afternoon carriage excursions, during which they talked about the future and made plans to travel when they left the presidency. Dismissing his overly loud escort at long last, Abraham told Mary cheerfully, "I prefer to ride by ourselves to day."

MRS. WIDOW LINCOLN

Sister in Grief

Arguably, the two most famous widows in the world during the nineteenth century were Mary Lincoln and Queen Victoria. Dubbed the "eternal widow of Windsor," Queen Victoria lost her Prince Consort in 1861, grieved in private for the next twenty years, and in all spent forty years ruling Great Britain in widow's weeds—the black of full mourning or at least half-mourning's violet and white. When President Lincoln died three and a half years later, Victoria wrote to his widow, Mary, that "No one can better appreciate than I can, who am myself utterly broken-hearted by the loss of my own beloved husband, who was the light of my life, my stay, my all, what your sufferings must be; and I earnestly pray that you may be supported by Him to Whom alone the sorely stricken can look for comfort, in this hour of heavy affliction!"

Victoria may have been right that, given the two widows' situations as British queen and American First Lady, she alone could understand Mary Lincoln's plight. Mary Lincoln agreed fully. Her two-sentence reply thanked the queen for her "expressions of tender sympathy, coming as they do, from a heart which from its own sorrow, can appreciate the *intense grief* I now endure." This simple exchange of letters gains poignancy when considered in the broader context of the two women's widowhood. Prince Albert had endured failing health for years, possibly suffering a peptic ulcer, Crohn's disease, or even stomach cancer. Albert's exhaustion attending to affairs of state in place of Victoria was heightened considerably by the outbreak of the American Civil War and particularly the Trent Affair that propelled the two nations perilously close to the brink of war. Throughout the Civil War, the British feared that any confrontation with the United States might lead to the loss of Canada. Speaking for Victoria, Albert strenuously counseled moderation to avert war with America. The memorandum that he wrote in his successful attempt to remain at peace with the Americans comprised his last official act, but the effort so exhausted him that he succumbed to typhoid fever and died in December 1861.

The American Civil War did not cost Albert his life, but it may well have hastened his decline. Now Victoria had to assume many of the weighty responsibilities that had led, indirectly, to her husband's death. Diplomatic tensions continued between the United States and Britain throughout the war. After Abraham Lincoln's assassination, Victoria's ministers advised her to send a letter of condolence to Mary Lincoln as a diplomatic gesture. They expected it to receive wide publicity and help heal the two countries' frosty relationship. In fact, in her grief, Mary Lincoln did not publicize the queen's letter at all and answered it in a mere two sentences. The British may not have fully understood that as a former First Lady, Mary Lincoln did not exercise any influence over the U.S. government, as the queen, of course, now did in her own widowhood. This was, in fact, the central distinction between the two widows. Victoria gained power, however reluctantly, when her husband Albert died. Mary Lincoln lost whatever power she might have possessed when her husband Abraham died. Victoria bemoaned the new responsibilities that fell upon her with Albert's death. Mary Lincoln bemoaned the profound neglect and indeed ridicule that she experienced at the hands of both the government and the American public once she left the White House.

Perhaps most important in the fleeting exchange between the two widows is the example of grief that Victoria set as a model for Mary Lincoln to emulate. Although the two women never met, in 1869 they came close to it when Mary Lincoln visited Scotland. Reaching Balmoral Castle, Mary discovered that "the Queen was absent," but in a letter home she reported that "I *have every* assurance, that as sisters in grief a warm welcome would be given me—*wherever* she is—yet I prefer quiet." In fact, Mary Lincoln assiduously followed the example of mourning that Queen Victoria had set before her. She began her sisterhood in grief as soon as Prince Albert died. Holding her lavish first reception at the White House in February 1862, she had decorated her white silk dress with "hundreds of black flounces" to express sympathy with Victoria. When her son Willie contracted typhoid fever that very night, the same disease that had claimed Albert two months earlier, the First Lady saw God's wrath at work as a punishment for her extravagance and heedless pride. When Willie died, Mary Lincoln joined Victoria in excessive mourning, reflecting the same spirit in which the queen's physician, Sir William Jenner, believed that she still suffered a "sort of madness" ten years into her widowhood.

With Willie's death, Mary Lincoln abandoned French empress Eugenie as her fashion exemplar in favor of Victoria, who was now renowned as "the high priestess of grief." Most conspicuously, Mary Lincoln banished all mementoes and acquaintances of Willie from the White House. (This was exactly the opposite reaction from Victoria. She kept Prince Albert's rooms intact, ordered his clothes laid out every morning with a basin of hot water and a towel, and lavished mementoes around her—including dozens of images of Albert—to celebrate his memory.) Emulating the queen, Mary Lincoln ordered lavish mourning regalia, black crepe dresses, bonnets, veils, and jewelry. She also emulated the queen in turning to spiritualism to reach Willie, just as Victoria was known to depend on psychics for emotional support. One American visitor reported that he heard "constant references to and jokes about 'Mrs Brown' . . . an English synonym for the Queen . . . I have been told that the Queen was insane, and John Brown was her keeper; that the Queen was a spiritualist, and John Brown was her medium." So when Abraham Lincoln died, his widow was prepared to mourn, indeed she was already in half-mourning.

Albert's funeral had been private, as were all royal funerals. In fact, there were calls for making an exception and allowing the public to attend Albert's funeral, but Victoria stood on royal tradition and refused. By contrast, presidential funerals are eminently public affairs, befitting the openness of a republican government. Abraham Lincoln received the grandest presidential funeral—probably the grandest funeral bar none—in American history. His funeral train, dubbed "The Lincoln Special," carried his body and 300 mourners on a circuitous, two-week, 1,654-mile journey through the North to his resting place in Springfield, Illinois, stopping in major cities along the way where thousands of mourners filed past his body. Americans boasted that their farewell to Lincoln put to shame the most notoriously lavish funeral in British history, the public remembrance of Lord Wellington in 1852. Through it all, Mary Lincoln grieved in private, for six weeks, refusing to leave the White House where she continued to reign, according to some observers, as a "Republican queen."

Practicing what her biographer Jean Baker has labeled "competitive mourning," Mary Lincoln followed Victoria's example and mourned for the rest of her life. She rejected the two-and-a-half years of mourning that most manuals recommended and for the remaining seventeen years of her life, she continued to wear the "first mourning" that most widows shed after the traditional year and a day. Only once in seventeen years did she abandon black crepe—on her son Tad's birthday—and wore instead black silk to celebrate that occasion. Even in mourning, however, she still insisted on following the fashions, traveling to New York and Boston, and now London and Paris as well, visiting dressmakers and spending lavishly on the latest fabrics. But instead of wearing them, she packed them up in trunks that she kept nearby at all times, as if to prove that she knew how to be fashionable but also to heighten the significance of the sacrifice embodied in her mourning attire. She eventually filled sixty-four trunks that she bore with her on even her most distant travels. At one point, Congress even held hearings to investigate the contents of her trunks.

Release

As time went on, Mary Lincoln gradually lost her few allies in both Springfield and Washington, and even her once reliable family members began to surrender their ties to her. Instead of returning to Springfield and the incessant reminders of her previous life with her husband and boys, she decided to move to Chicago with her remaining sons. She could not bear the thought of revisiting the house on Eighth and Jackson with all of its memories. "After many years of happiness there with my idolized husband," she insisted, "to place me in the home deprived of *his* presence and the darling boy we lost in Washington, it would not require a day, for me to lose my entire reason." Abraham Lincoln's estate contained $85,000, representing most of his annual salary ($25,000) from his first term as president. David Davis, the estate's administrator, however, concealed that figure, providing a relatively meager $1,500 a year to each of the president's three survivors and postponing settlement of the estate for three years. Mary was forced to undertake an extended pilgrimage from one hotel to the next in a continual effort to trim expenses. Robert apprenticed in a law firm downtown and soon decided to move on to a place of his own. Tad enrolled in a private academy, the first school he ever attended.

Now the eastern merchants who had courted her as First Lady began demanding payment and even threatening to sue her to satisfy the outstanding debt of perhaps $10,000 that she had managed to conceal from her husband up to the very end. She began returning items for partial refunds but refused to give up a 508-piece set of imported china that she had ordered from a mercantile house in Philadelphia. She bemoaned her plight as a neglected and unappreciated widow and hired an agent in the Treasury Department to solicit donations from wealthy Republicans. Potential donors, however, were reluctant to contribute even to Lincoln's widow when her renowned extravagance not only continued but even escalated, relative to her actual needs, after she left the White House. Meanwhile, David Davis discouraged contributions by privately assuring her friends that she didn't need the money. Congress eventually awarded her the fifth year of Lincoln's presidential salary, which she used to pay for a comfortable house on Chicago's West Side. Still, she could not manage the home on the $1,500 a year that Davis provided, so she rented it out for the income and eventually had to sell it.

Robert Lincoln, Abraham and Mary Lincoln's eldest son, at the close of the Civil War; carte de visite from photograph taken by Mathew Brady around 1865. Library of Congress.

Now, Mary Lincoln and Elizabeth Keckly devised a plan to sell the wardrobe that she had accumulated during her years in the White House for what they hoped would amount to $100,000. Predictably, when the items went on display in New York the press sensationalized and mocked what they labeled "Mrs. Lincoln's Second-hand Clothing Sale." As historian Jean Baker has emphasized, Mary Lincoln equated her fine and expensive wardrobe with her own self-worth. When the public, including former friends and White House supplicants, rejected the clothing as worn, gaudy, and even ill-gotten, she received a devastating blow to her insatiable need for approval and her always vulnerable sense of acceptance. Partisan opponents and even former Confederates sneered that she was putting the evidence of the Lincoln administration's susceptibility to bribery on brazen display.

In a touching attempt to help, Elizabeth Keckly enlisted the aid of African American leaders who appreciated the former First Lady's support for contraband relief during the war. African American leaders, including Lincoln's friend Frederick Douglass, offered to organize a lecture tour with all of the fees going to Mary. Ungratefully, Mary Lincoln refused their help. She ultimately abandoned Keckly, her last close friend and confidante, when the seamstress published a book, *Behind the Scenes: Thirty Years a Slave and Four Years in the White House*, which she presented as a novel but everyone considered a memoir. As her biographer Jean Baker observed, "After the old clothes sale she had become one of the most unpopular women in America." Mary now vowed to leave behind "this ungrateful Republic" for Europe, where Tad and she traveled together for the next three years. In a final, tragic misfortune from which she never really recovered, Mary's last faithful companion, her youngest son Tad, contracted a lung disease, possibly tuberculosis, during their ocean voyage home from Europe. He suffered for two months and then died, at age eighteen in July 1871. By age fifty-two, Mary Lincoln had seen her husband and three of her four sons die, realizing a wife and mother's worst fears four times over, in little more than two decades.

As her behavior grew increasingly eccentric, her only surviving family member, her son Robert, obtained a warrant for her arrest on the grounds of lunacy. A thorough and methodical lawyer, Robert Lincoln hired Pinkerton detectives to conduct surveillance of his mother's actions, consulted physicians to testify to her mental condition, and obtained witnesses who could describe her strange behavior in detail. In May 1875, without warning, Leonard Swett, a lawyer and longtime family friend, arrived at her door and presented her with the warrant and the choice of going to the Cook County Courthouse immediately, either voluntarily or involuntarily. Swett would not even allow her to change her clothes. Mary went voluntarily and at the courthouse discovered that Robert and David Davis had orchestrated the proceeding in response to her "delusional" belief in spiritualism, her "excessive" mourning over the deaths of her husband and son Tad, and what they considered her wanton overspending. During the trial, which took place that very afternoon, five physicians testified that Mary Lincoln was insane, based solely on Robert's descriptions of her behavior. Eleven additional witnesses, including hotel employees and salesclerks, testified to her eccentric actions. The final witness was Robert himself, who took the stand to tell the court that "I have no doubt that my mother is insane." After deliberating for ten minutes, the jury issued a verdict of insanity and sentenced her to a mental institution.

Mary Lincoln served just under four months in Bellevue Place sanatorium, a private and exclusive medical facility in Batavia, Illinois. Her strategy was two-fold. First, she behaved perfectly normally during her entire incarceration, despite several sensational but scurrilous press reports to the contrary. Second, she obtained the help of Myra Bradwell, the first woman ever admitted to the Illinois bar as a lawyer. Bradwell, who was an advocate for women's rights, and her husband James, a lawyer, judge, and state legislator, launched a publicity campaign to bring Mary's plight to the attention of the public, along with a simultaneous legal campaign to win her release. In open defiance of Robert Lincoln, the superintendent of Bellevue Place released Mary Lincoln on the condition that she "secure a quiet home for herself." Mary had outwitted Robert and his team of doctors and lawyers. Her eldest sister, Elizabeth Edwards, agreed to take her into her home, the same house on "Aristocrat's Hill" where she had courted and won Abraham Lincoln as her own thirty-five years earlier.

Lincoln biographers have generally portrayed Robert, in historian Jason Emerson's words, as "a rapacious, avaricious, coldhearted snob who detested his mother and put her away to rid himself of her and steal her money." The recent discovery of two caches of legal papers documenting her commitment and release, however, have tempered this image of Robert Lincoln as duplicitous, callous, and self-serving. In 1975, the Illinois state historian, James Hickey, uncovered Robert Lincoln's personal records of the case in a safe in the bedroom closet of his home, Hildene, in Manchester, Vermont. Thirty years later, Jason Emerson discovered extensive correspondence between Mary Lincoln and her defenders in an attic in a trunk that once belonged to Robert Lincoln's lawyer. After analyzing all of the newly available evidence, Emerson has concluded that Mary Lincoln suffered from early stages of bipolar disorder accompanied by depression, delusions, hallucinations, mood swings, and pathological overspending, or monomania. If so, then Robert Lincoln's actions, no matter how callously they were carried out, were designed not merely to win control of his mother's inheritance, preserve the dignity and privacy of the Lincoln family, or exercise an extreme patriarchal dominance over an independent, strong-willed, and outspoken woman. Robert Lincoln was trying to protect his mother from herself. At wit's end, he considered the highly irregular legal proceeding that he orchestrated a necessary last resort.

While Queen Victoria's and Mary Lincoln's situations—and behavior—exhibited many similarities, their essential distinction is obvious. On Albert's death, Victoria remained queen. On Abraham Lincoln's death, Mary Lincoln lost her status as First Lady. Victoria's status as constitutional monarch allowed her to grieve excessively, prompting sympathy and even admiration. Mary Lincoln's loss of status as First Lady (of a republic) undoubtedly compounded the complexity of her grief. In Britain, politicians and the public exhorted Queen Victoria for decades to resume her involvement in public affairs. In America, politicians and the public reviled Mary Lincoln for her attempts to remain engaged in politics and, particularly, to wrest a pension from the government. Parliament cheerfully increased its subsidies to the Crown as Victoria's nine children reached adulthood and reared families of their own. Congress bitterly resisted a pension for Mary Lincoln through her first fifteen years of campaigning and lobbying. Finally, after President James Garfield's assassination in 1881, Congress decided to award *his* widow a pension of $5,000 and at last gave in to Mary Lincoln's pleas, providing $5,000 a year plus $15,000 in back payments. The sole dissenter in Congress labeled the pension aristocratic and unrepublican, and before receiving it, Mary had to be examined by four doctors to certify that she was disabled and could not work. Three other presidential widows—Sarah Polk, Julia Grant, and Lucretia Garfield—received pensions at the same time. However, Mary Lincoln died six months later in the house on "Aristocrat's Hill" and never received a penny, after seventeen years of widowhood—and four years of service as First Lady of a divided nation at war against itself.

CONCLUSION: AN AMERICAN UNION

Mary Lincoln was tremendously helpful, even instrumental, in her husband's rise to the American presidency. Fueling his ambition, maintaining a stable home life for his family, entertaining lavishly both at Eighth and Jackson and in the White House, doing what she could to polish her husband's manners, and lending her family's political credentials, connections, and influence to his early career—in a multitude of ways, Mary Lincoln was an asset to the rising young lawyer and politician. For many of these same reasons, however, she became a liability during his presidency. Her political and social ambitions, which she had always fused with her husband's, were inappropriate in the White House, certainly in the midst of the sectional division and the grievous human sacrifices occasioned by the Civil War. The ever-present Todd in-laws, and even her Edwards and Stuart connections, created complications for the chief executive as he directed the war and led the Republican Party. Her reaction to the death of Willie, her overprotectiveness of Robert, and even her indulgence toward mischievous Tad, all of which Lincoln himself forgave, proved detrimental to the president. Even when she left Washington to travel, shop, and recuperate, her best-intentioned actions proved counterproductive. Always constrained by the prescriptive limits of domesticity, Mary Lincoln consistently pushed back against its boundaries, and never more so, and more conspicuously, than in Washington.

Always different, even opposites, in character, temperament, and personality, Abraham and Mary Lincoln exemplified the stereotypical gender roles that defined American marriages during the nineteenth century and that were always intended to complement each other. Balancing false alternatives—reason and emotion, thought and action, competitiveness and compassion, public and private, work and family—promoted a constant struggle within the Lincolns' marriage that exposed, and in the White House came to embody, on a national stage, all of these enduring cultural contradictions. Ever a man of the middle, Abraham Lincoln could always forge a compromise that acknowledged the justice that lay within both ends of the spectrum. Ever a woman of extremes, Mary Lincoln succumbed to all of these unrealistic prescriptions in her effort to craft a typical marital union with an extraordinary man. But what a fascinating and enigmatic marriage they forged in undertaking it.

ACKNOWLEDGMENTS

ESSAY ON SOURCES

BIBLIOGRAPHY

INDEX

ACKNOWLEDGMENTS

During the years that I have devoted to researching and writing about the Lincoln family, many people and institutions have kindly offered encouragement, advice, and support. At the University of Nebraska–Lincoln, Vice Chancellor for Research and Economic Development Prem S. Paul, Dean David Manderscheid of the College of Arts and Sciences, Dean Joan Giesecke of University Libraries, the UNL Research Council, the Center for Digital Research in the Humanities, and the Department of History have generously provided funding for documentary materials, computing equipment, travel, and research assistance. The digital project that I codirect at UNL with Kenneth Price and Susan Lawrence, *Civil War Washington*, has recently received substantial funding from the National Endowment for the Humanities through a three-year Collaborative Research Grant that carries "We the People" designation, which will support continued investigation of Washington, D.C., during the Civil War era. Beyond this indispensable institutional support, dozens of archivists and librarians at depositories across the country have generously contributed their time, energy, and insights to the never-ending search for source material. The most important archives for my research include the Illinois State Historical Library, the Illinois Historic Preservation Agency, the Abraham Lincoln Presidential Library and Museum, the Abraham Lincoln Papers, and the Sangamon Valley Collection of the Lincoln Library, all located in Springfield, Illinois, and the Library of Congress and the National Archives in Washington, D.C. The Illinois State Historian, Dr. Thomas F. Schwartz, merits special recognition for his renowned willingness to share his knowledge and expertise generously and enthusiastically among Lincoln scholars. For the present volume, the Abraham Lincoln Presidential Library and Museum and the Library of Congress kindly granted permission to reproduce photographs from their collections.

The editors of the Concise Lincoln Library—Richard W. Etulain, Sara Vaughn Gabbard, and Sylvia Frank Rodrigue—have been insightful and imaginative in their conception of this series of succinct contributions to Lincoln studies, for which I feel honored to provide a volume. Throughout the long process of the research, writing, and revision that has culminated in *Abraham and Mary Lincoln*, the editors, as well as the anonymous referee, have provided expert and perceptive advice, along with a generous dose of collegial support, all of which I genuinely appreciate. Southern Illinois University Press has been equally rewarding to work with in all respects.

Among the many outstanding Lincoln scholars and Civil War historians who have generously provided encouragement, advice, and help over the past two decades, this book's dedication recognizes my gratitude to one of the finest.

ESSAY ON SOURCES

The most important resources for examining and interpreting Abraham and Mary Lincoln's marriage are, of course, their own words, to the extent that they have survived and are available to scholars. The essential source for any study of Abraham Lincoln is Roy P. Basler's nine-volume *Collected Works of Abraham Lincoln* (1953), whose appearance facilitated the scholarly reconsideration of Lincoln's life and professional and political careers during the second half of the twentieth century. A searchable, digital edition of Lincoln's collected works, which includes more recently discovered documents and incoming correspondence, is available through the Library of Congress and the Lincoln Studies Center (http://memory.loc.gov/ammem/alhtml/malhome.html). When complete, the Papers of Abraham Lincoln (http://papersofabrahamlincoln.org) will provide access to all documents written by or to Lincoln as both images and searchable transcriptions. Mary Lincoln's letters are scarcer, so we are more dependent on the observations of others to reconstruct her life. Her outgoing letters are reprinted and interpreted in Justin G. Turner and Linda Levitt Turner's invaluable *Mary Todd Lincoln: Her Life and Letters* (1987). Jason Emerson's *The Madness of Mary Lincoln* (2007) reprints and analyzes a cache of Mary Lincoln's recently discovered correspondence.

A wealth of primary observations survive in the form of contemporary letters, diaries, and newspapers reports. Most valuable for reconstructing the married life of the Lincolns are Elizabeth Keckly's memoir, *Behind the Scenes in the White House* (orig. pub. 1868), John Hay's *Inside Lincoln's White House* (1997), William O. Stoddard's *Inside the White House in War Times* (2000), Walt Whitman's *Specimen Days* (1882–83), and Katherine Helm's *True Story of Mary, Wife of Lincoln* (1928). Each views its subject from a unique perspective. Michael Burlingame's magisterial two-volume biography, *Abraham Lincoln: A Life* (2008), presents a trove of contemporary observations about both Lincolns. A lengthier, unpublished version of Burlingame's biography that includes additional observations and details is available online at http://www.knox.edu/Academics/Distinctive-

Programs/Lincoln-Studies-Center/Burlingame-Abraham-Lincoln-A-Life.html. Mark Neely and R. Gerald McMurtry's *Insanity File* (1986) analyzes Robert Lincoln's perspective on his mother's institutionalization through a recently discovered deposit of his personal records. Among contemporary newspapers, the *Illinois State Journal* in Springfield and the *National Republican* in Washington were most sympathetic toward the Lincolns.

Recollections and reminiscences produced and collected after Abraham Lincoln's death represent the largest and most controversial body of evidence documenting the couple's marriage. Soon after Lincoln's assassination, his longtime law partner, William Herndon, began offering his own reminiscences and compiling the recollections of others through a decades-long oral history project that culminated in his 1889 biography. Within a mere eighteen months of Lincoln's death, the letters that Herndon had solicited and collected and the interviews that he had conducted and recorded totaled more than four hundred. Through his commitment to compiling extensive documentation through the firsthand reminiscences of people who knew the Lincolns, Herndon made invaluable contributions to both the content and methodology of all subsequent Lincoln scholarship. Much of what we know about the Lincolns' personal lives, particularly during the period preceding the presidency, originated from Herndon and his collection of letters and reminiscences.

Regrettably, however, Herndon had experienced a distant and even frosty relationship with Mary Lincoln, and she did not fare well in his writing nor in other biographical accounts that drew on his enormous collection of reminiscences. Herndon disclosed a bias against Mary Lincoln almost immediately after his law partner's death in a series of lectures that he delivered in Springfield in 1865 and 1866. While praising Abraham Lincoln's public character, conduct, and accomplishments, Herndon portrayed him personally as gloomy, pessimistic, and—through a lifelong religious skepticism—fatalistic. In his fourth and final lecture, Herndon identified Lincoln's relationship with Ann Rutledge as an important source of this purported melancholy. Arguing that "Abraham Lincoln loved Miss Ann Rutledge with all his soul, mind and strength," Herndon concluded that after her death he never truly loved another woman, including his wife. Overall, he portrayed the couple's marriage as stormy, dysfunctional, and, on Abraham Lincoln's part, loveless.

Robert Lincoln visited Springfield in a futile attempt to convince Herndon to retract his assertions and, along with David Davis and others close to his mother, managed to shield her from the unwelcome revelations for four months. When at last Mary Lincoln read the lecture in March 1867, her attitude toward Herndon changed at once from diffidence to abhorrence. "This is the return for all my husband's kindness to this miserable man!" she wrote bitterly. She resented what she considered Herndon's "infamous falsehoods" and labeled the Ann Rutledge episode, in particular, a "pathetic & sensational love story," indeed a "myth." She characterized Herndon himself as her husband's "crazy drinking law partner," a "renowned scamp & humbug," and even a "dirty dog." For his part, Herndon retaliated by labeling Lincoln's widow a "she-wolf," a "wild cat," and a "liar," and he helped to fuel the growing public and private perception that she was insane. Subsequent biographers have suggested that Herndon's animosity toward Mary Lincoln led him, either intentionally or inadvertently, to elicit unflattering reminiscences about her from his oral history respondents.

The legacy of Herndon's lectures, biography, and collection of reminiscences was a strong strain of negative sentiment toward Mary Lincoln that dominated Lincoln scholarship for over a century and still persists to this day. In the mid-twentieth century, a growing insistence on objectivity and professionalism in the field of Lincoln studies led a new generation of scholars, including James G. Randall, David Donald, and Ruth Painter Randall, to reject not only Herndon's portrayal of a loveless Lincoln marriage and a venomous Mary Lincoln but also the validity of the reminiscences that supported this interpretation. In 1945, James G. Randall wrote an influential essay that challenged the value of the reminiscences that Herndon had so assiduously compiled and even questioned the existence of the love affair between Abraham Lincoln and Ann Rutledge. "Assuredly the effect of the episode upon Lincoln's later life," Randall concluded, "has been greatly exaggerated—or rather, fabricated." In 1948, David

Donald followed up with a biography of Herndon that portrayed him as an influential but flawed biographer who uncovered a great deal of important information about the Lincolns but also contributed questionable myths informed by personal biases. Donald labeled Herndon simultaneously a "myth-maker and truth-teller" and concluded that "One of the most important things about Herndon is the errors that he spread." This scholarly reassessment of Herndon's legacy facilitated a resurgence of interest in Mary Lincoln that sought a balanced understanding informed by verifiable evidence and grounded in historical context. The result was a far fuller, more objective, and more favorable portrait, exemplified by Ruth Painter Randall's *Mary Lincoln: Biography of a Marriage* (1953), which among other innovations labeled the Ann Rutledge episode a "fictitious romance."

Subsequent biographers of both Lincolns have striven for greater objectivity, denser documentation, and broader contextualization. In 1987, historian Jean H. Baker produced the consummate biography of Mary Lincoln in this balanced vein, acknowledging her flaws but also analyzing them objectively and systematically within the social, cultural, and sexual context of nineteenth-century America and the demands and expectations that circumscribed Victorian marriages. In a subsequent essay in *The Lincoln Enigma* (2001), Baker labeled the Lincolns' marriage "A Union of Opposites," in which the partners "complemented each other—not in the ancient way of marriage as a little commonwealth with the husband and father as ruler and the wife and mother as subject." Instead, both Lincolns imbibed "the companionate ideal of a new closeness of husband and wife—the 'tender passion' of a nineteenth-century marital style based on difference."

Simultaneously, Lincoln biographers returned to reminiscences as a vital and increasingly accessible, if often unreliable and contradictory, source of important insights. Framing their use within a new sensitivity to the personal biases, memory lapses, and other imperfections that can afflict oral history collections, scholars have restored reminiscences to a vital, secondary role within the hierarchy of tools available for writing biography and analyzing the past. The annotation and publication of Herndon's collection of letters and reminiscences as *Herndon's Informants* (1998), which is available in searchable format online (http://durer.press.illinois.edu/wilson/ html/737.html), has stimulated a surge of similar efforts to locate, edit, and disseminate untapped stores of oral testimony that have lain long forgotten. One of the most conspicuous results has been historians' new respect for Ann Rutledge's death as a crucial formative episode in Abraham Lincoln's development, although not a primary factor in his relationship with his wife Mary. Reminiscences, carefully considered in context and weighed against competing evidence, now inform and enliven the best Lincoln biographies. Michael Burlingame's *Abraham Lincoln: A Life* (2008) is noteworthy in this respect.

Overall, recent biographers have devoted more analysis to Lincoln's private, family life as an important and generally positive contributor to his character, his behavior, and indeed his professional success as a lawyer, politician, and president. Mary Lincoln has accordingly gained renewed importance as a biographical subject. Fine examples of this recent scholarship include David Donald's *Lincoln* (1995), Jennifer Fleischner's *Mrs. Lincoln and Mrs. Keckly* (2003), Ronald White's *A. Lincoln: A Biography* (2009), and Catherine Clinton's *Mrs. Lincoln: A Life* (2009). Our broadest goal in reading and writing biography is to improve our understanding of the social, cultural, political, and economic context in which individual lives unfolded. Recent studies that employ the Lincolns' lives to enhance our knowledge of the Civil War Era more generally include Matthew Pinsker's *Lincoln's Sanctuary: Abraham Lincoln and the Soldiers' Home* (2003), *Our Lincoln: New Perspectives on Lincoln and His World*, edited by Eric Foner (2008), and *Abraham Lincoln's America*, edited by Joseph Fornieri and Sara Gabbard (2008).

BIBLIOGRAPHY

Jean H. Baker, "Mary and Abraham: A Marriage," in *The Lincoln Enigma: The Changing Faces of an American Icon*, ed. Gabor Boritt. New York: Oxford University Press, 2001.

———, *Mary Todd Lincoln: A Biography*. New York: W. W. Norton, 1987.

Roy P. Basler et al., eds., *The Collected Works of Abraham Lincoln*. 9 vols. New Brunswick, N.J.: Rutgers University Press, 1953–55.

Julia Taft Bayne, *Tad Lincoln's Father*. Lincoln: University of Nebraska Press, 2001 (orig. pub. 1931).

Stephen Berry, *House of Abraham: Lincoln and the Todds, A Family Divided by War*. New York: Houghton Mifflin, 2007.

Elizabeth Smith Brownstein, *Lincoln's Other White House: The Untold Story of the Man and His Presidency*. New York: Wiley, 2005.

Michael Burlingame, *Abraham Lincoln: A Life*. 2 vols. Baltimore: Johns Hopkins University Press, 2008.

———, *The Inner World of Abraham Lincoln*. Urbana: University of Illinois Press, 1994.

Michael Burlingame and John R. Turner Ettlinger, eds., *Inside Lincoln's White House: The Complete Civil War Diary of John Hay*. Carbondale: Southern Illinois University Press, 1997.

Catherine Clinton, *Mrs. Lincoln: A Life*. New York: Harper, 2009.

Rodney O. Davis, *Abraham Lincoln: Son and Father*. Galesburg, Ill.: The Edgar S. and Ruth W. Burkhardt Lecture Series, Knox College, 1997.

David Donald, *Lincoln's Herndon*. New York: Alfred A. Knopf, 1948.

David Herbert Donald, *Lincoln*. New York: Simon & Schuster, 1995.

———, *Lincoln at Home: Two Glimpses of Abraham Lincoln's Family Life*. New York: Simon & Schuster, 1999.

———, *"We Are Lincoln Men": Abraham Lincoln and His Friends*. New York: Simon & Schuster, 2003.

Jason Emerson, *The Madness of Mary Lincoln*. Carbondale: Southern Illinois University Press, 2007.

Daniel Mark Epstein, *Lincoln's Men: The President and His Private Secretaries*. New York: Collins, 2009.

———. *The Lincolns: Portrait of a Marriage*. New York: Ballantine Books, 2008.

Jennifer Fleischner, *Mrs. Lincoln and Mrs. Keckly*. New York: Broadway Books, 2003.

Eric Foner, ed., *Our Lincoln: New Perspectives on Lincoln and His World*. New York: W. W. Norton, 2008.

Joseph F. Fornieri and Sara Vaughn Gabbard, eds., *Abraham Lincoln's America, 1809–1865*. Carbondale: Southern Illinois University Press, 2008.

Katherine Helm, *The True Story of Mary, Wife of Lincoln*. New York: Harper & Brothers, 1928.

William H. Herndon and Jesse W. Weik, *Herndon's Lincoln*, ed. Douglas L. Wilson and Rodney O. Davis. Urbana: University of Illinois Press, 2006 (orig. pub. 1889).

Patricia Jalland, *Death in the Victorian Family*. New York: Oxford University Press, 1996.

Michael W. Kauffman, *American Brutus: John Wilkes Booth and the Lincoln Conspiracies*. New York: Random House, 2004.

Elizabeth Keckley, *Behind the Scenes in the Lincoln White House: Memoirs of an African-American Seamstress*. Mineola, N.Y.: Dover Publications, 2006 (orig. pub. 1868).

Ward Hill Lamon, *Recollections of Abraham Lincoln, 1847–1865*. Lincoln: University of Nebraska Press, 1994 (orig. pub. 1872).

Christopher Lasch, *Haven in a Heartless World: The Family Besieged*. New York: Basic Books, 1977.

Karen Lystra, *Searching the Heart: Women, Men, and Romantic Love in Nineteenth-Century America*. New York: Oxford University Press, 1989.

Mark E. Neely Jr. and Harold Holzer, *The Lincoln Family Album*. New York: Doubleday, 1990.

Mark E. Neely and R. Gerald McMurtry, *The Insanity File: The Case of Mary Todd Lincoln*. Carbondale: Southern Illinois University Press, 1986.

Jerrold M. Packard, *The Lincolns in the White House*. New York: St. Martin's Griffin, 2005.

Matthew Pinsker, *Lincoln's Sanctuary: Abraham Lincoln and the Soldiers' Home*. New York: Oxford University Press, 2003.

J. G. Randall, *Lincoln the President: Springfield to Gettysburg*. New York: Dodd, Mead, 1945.

Ruth Painter Randall, *Mary Lincoln: Biography of a Marriage*. Boston: Little, Brown, 1953.

Ronald D. Rietveld, "The Lincoln White House Community," *Journal of the Abraham Lincoln Association* 20 (Summer 1999), 17–48.

Ellen K. Rothman, *Hands and Hearts: A History of Courtship in America*. New York: Basic Books, 1984.

William Seale, *The President's House: A History*. 2 vols. Washington, D.C.: White House Historical Association, 1986.

William O. Stoddard, *Inside the White House in War Times: Memoirs and Reports of Lincoln's Secretary*, ed. Michael Burlingame. Lincoln: University of Nebraska Press, 2000.

Justin G. Turner and Linda Levitt Turner, *Mary Todd Lincoln: Her Life and Letters*. New York: Fromm International Publishing, 1987.

John E. Washington, *They Knew Lincoln*. New York: E. P. Dutton, 1942.

Tom Wheeler, *Mr. Lincoln's T-Mails: The Untold Story of How Abraham Lincoln Used the Telegraph to Win the Civil War.* New York: Collins, 2006.

Ronald C. White Jr., *A. Lincoln: A Biography.* New York: Random House, 2009.

Walt Whitman, *Specimen Days.* Philadelphia: R. Welsh & Co., 1882–83.

Douglas L. Wilson and Rodney O. Davis, eds., *Herndon's Informants: Letters, Interviews, and Statements about Abraham Lincoln.* Urbana: University of Illinois Press, 1998.

Kenneth J. Winkle, *The Young Eagle: The Rise of Abraham Lincoln.* Dallas: Taylor Publishers, 2001.

INDEX

Italicized page numbers refer to figures. Abraham Lincoln is referred to in subheadings as AL.

McClellan, George, 111–12

McNamar, John (McNeil), 30–31, 32

Mendonsa, Antonio, 52

Mexican War, 70–71

middle class, new: dinner parties of, 52–53; family size, 54–55; gender roles in, 49–52, 54, 59–64; industrialization and, 48–50; values and standards of, 48, 50–52, 54, 60–64, 100

migrations, 3–4, 6, 13, 25–28

milk sickness, 8

Missouri Compromise, 74

Mrs. Sprigg's boardinghouse, 70, 72

Napoleon, Prince, on White House visit, 84

New Orleans slave market, 66

New Salem, Illinois, 21–23, 30–35

New York Calvary Regiment, 11th, 113

New York Volunteer Infantry, 11th, 83

Nicolay, John: on friendship of AL and Speed, 36; Mary Lincoln and, 95–96, 99; rail journey to Washington, D.C., 77; at Tuesday evening levee, 105; White House offices and accommodation, 87, 88

Northwest Ordinance, 67

office seekers, 87–88

Offutt, Denten, 66

Ohio River, as boundary, 5

One-Legged Brigade, 80

Owens, Mary, 33–35

pardon seekers, 87–88

Parker, Eliza. See Todd, Elizabeth "Eliza" Parker

Parker family, 11–12

pavilion hospitals, 79–80

pensions, for widows of presidents, 123–24

Pigeon Creek home, Indiana, 8, 13

Polk, Sarah, 124

Pomroy, Rebecca, 85

popular sovereignty, 74

Potomac River, as water source and sewer, 85, 91–92

Powell, Beverly, 45

prairie agriculture, 20

presidential funerals, 117–18

prisons, 80

"Rebecca Letters," 44–45

Republican Party, emergence in Illinois, 74

Rockingham County, Virginia, 4

Rodney, Anna, 45

Rodney, Caesar, 45

Roundtree, Lucy, 67

royal funerals, 117–18

Rutledge, Ann, 30–35

Rutledge, James, 30

Rutledge, Polly, 29, 30

Rutledge, Robert, 22, 30–31

Sangamon County, Illinois, 29–30, 65–66

Sangamon Journal, 69

sanitation, in the White House, 91–92

Scott, Winfield, 82

Scottish Covenanters, 9

séances, 101

sex ratio imbalances, 29–30, 36–37

Shawnee people, 5

Shearer, Hannah, 102

Shelby Female Academy, 17

Shenandoah River, 4

Shields, James, 44

Slade, Katherine "Nibbie," 89

Slade, William, 86, 109

slavery: AL's antislavery principles, 66–69, 71–72, 74; AL's initiation to, 19; Lincoln family and, 6–7; sectional crisis over, 70–71; in

Kenneth J. Winkle received his PhD at the University of Wisconsin–Madison and is the Sorensen Professor of American History at the University of Nebraska–Lincoln. His three prize-winning books in the field of nineteenth-century U.S. political, social, cultural, and military history—*The Politics of Community: Migration and Politics in Antebellum Ohio* (1988), *The Young Eagle: The Rise of Abraham Lincoln* (2001), and *The Oxford Atlas of the Civil War* (2004)—received the Abraham Lincoln Institute Book Award, the Society for Military History's Distinguished Book Award, and the Allan Sharlin Award of the Social Science History Association. Winkle has published twenty articles and essays in the *Journal of Social History*, the *Journal of Interdisciplinary History*, *Civil War History*, *History Teacher*, the *Journal of the Abraham Lincoln Association*, *Social Science History*, *Reviews in American History*, the *Lincoln Newsletter*, and other publications. He is currently writing a book about Lincoln and his family in Washington, D.C., during the Civil War.

CONCISE
LINCOLN
LIBRARY

This series of concise books fills a need for short studies of the life, times, and legacy of President Abraham Lincoln. Each book gives readers the opportunity to quickly achieve basic knowledge of a Lincoln-related topic. These books bring fresh perspectives to well-known topics, investigate previously overlooked subjects, and explore in greater depth topics that have not yet received book-length treatment. For a complete list of current and forthcoming titles, see www.conciselincolnlibrary.com.

Other Books in the Concise Lincoln Library

Abraham Lincoln and Horace Greeley
Gregory A. Borchard

Abraham Lincoln and the Civil War
Michael Burlingame

Lincoln and the Election of 1860
Michael S. Green